NOT GOOD IF DETACHED

NOT GOOD
IF DETACHED

By

CORRIE TEN BOOM

CHRISTIAN LITERATURE CRUSADE
Fort Washington, Pennsylvania 19034

CHRISTIAN LITERATURE CRUSADE

CANADA
1440 Mackay Street, Montreal, Quebec

GREAT BRITAIN
The Dean, Alresford, Hampshire

AUSTRALIA
P.O. Box 91, Pennant Hills, N.S.W. 2120

NEW ZEALAND
Box 1688, Auckland, C.1

Also in:

Europe - Africa - South America - India
Philippines - Thailand - New Guinea
Pakistan - Indonesia - Japan
Caribbean Area

SBN 87508-0 22-7

Copyright © 1957
CHRISTIAN LITERATURE CRUSADE
London

First published 1957
First American Edition 1970

CONTENTS

CONTENTS

PREFACE

CORRIE TEN BOOM is one of those rare souls whose experience with God has been so different from that of other Christians that it must be described as unique. Brought up in the staid surroundings of a Reformed household and church in the Netherlands, her life was uneventful. Came the War, and Corrie with her family decided to succour the helpless Jewish victims of Gestapo terror without stopping to count the cost to herself. Had she known that it would take the lives of her nearest and dearest, she might have flinched. So merciful Providence hid the future from her, until she could live it one day at a time.

In *A Prisoner and Yet* . . . she tells of her walk with God through the valley of the shadow of an imminent death in Ravensbrück concentration camp. When unexpectedly released, a living skeleton, she quietly determined to carry out her vow to witness around the world to the grace of God.

Amazing Love tells of her post-war experiences far afield, and shows the maturing of her Christian service. It has been my privilege to know Corrie ten Boom and her ministry for several years, and a greater privilege still to have had her as a true yoke-fellow in the ministry in several of the continents. I do not know of anyone more earnestly seeking to be "one hundred per cent for God"—which is her own phrase to describe a fully-yielded life.

This book is written in Corrie's own style. Although her friends agree that she is always willing to learn, there are certain things that they cease trying to change; one of them being Corrie's style of writing and utterance. It is her own, and it is unique. It reflects her mind and her heart.

I commend to you our sister Corrie, a servant of the Church at large, that you may receive her in the Lord as befits the saints, and help her in whatever she may require from you, for she has been a helper of many and of myself as well.

In connection with this book, all that Corrie ten Boom requires of the reader is that this volume be read with a heart open for blessing.

J. Edwin Orr

April 1957

CHAPTER I

THREE AFRICAN BOYS

The world is our mission-field, for it is Jesus' mission-field.

IN a prison in Africa, forty boys are sitting on the concrete floor of their cell. They listen while I tell them about the promise of the Second Coming of Jesus. After a meeting in the prison square, they had asked to hear more. There they had been sitting with all the prisoners packed closely together, hundreds of boys, most of them younger than eighteen years, and many guilty of theft or murder. I had told them how Jesus lifted us up out of sin and death when He died for us. I barely mentioned the future, when this world shall be full of the knowledge of the Lord, as the waters cover the sea (Isa. 11 : 9). When Jesus comes, He has promised He will "make all things new" (Rev. 21 : 5).

The boys sleep on the cold floor of the cell. One boy puts his blanket on the little stool where I am to sit. It is all he possesses. An evangelist who regularly works among them is my interpreter, and he leads the prayer meeting which follows.

Several boys pray.

A sunbeam touches the face of a boy who prays on his knees, with his head uplifted. There is the peace that passes all understanding on his black face. He is seventeen years old, and was the leader of a gang.

In a small crowded prison Christians who bravely dare to witness have a difficult life. He is one who witnesses. I do not understand his language. Does he pray, "Come, Lord Jesus, come quickly"?

When leaving, I tell him and two others, "Just imagine that you saw Jesus coming there on those clouds up in heaven." There is longing and expectation on their eager faces when they look up.

There is coming a moment in history when that which is written of in Revelation 22 : 17 will take place, "And the Spirit and the bride say, 'Come.' And let him that heareth

say, 'Come.' And let him that is athirst come. And whosoever will, let him take the water of life freely."

I am called to distribute that "water of life" in many
countries.

In this book you will read about what God did with one
of His children on several trips throughout the world. The
experiences are so personal that the dangerous word "I" is
used too often. But it is my only wish to seek to honour Him
who is my Lord, Jesus Christ, God's Son.

The branch of the vine can only give fruit through Him.
Without Him we can do nothing. The riches in Him are so
great and full of joy. He is the only answer to the problem
of the hearts of men.

But we have this treasure in a "common earthenware
jar"—to show that the splendid power of it belongs to God
and not to us. For it is Christ the Lord whom we preach,
and not ourselves (2 Cor. 4 : 7, 5, Phillips).

In this book are told some of the things that happened to
a "common earthenware jar". It is the treasure that is important, not the jar.

At the time of writing this book I have been travelling for
ten years. Up to my fiftieth year I had always lived in one
town—Haarlem, in the Netherlands. Then the cruel hand
of war destroyed the quiet life of our happy family. The
foundation of our happiness was that we knew ourselves
hidden with Christ in God. The enemy could take away our
material possessions, but he could not destroy our faith in
God's love in Jesus Christ.

On the contrary, when all earthly security was very uncertain, we experienced with tremendous joy the invinci-
bility of the sure Rock to which our anchor is eternally
fastened. Before, we had believed, but now we knew that the
light of Jesus Christ is stronger than the deepest darkness.

First there were the years of intensive work in the underground movement to save Jewish people. Then came the
arrest and imprisonment of my whole family which, for all
except myself, ended in death. For me it ended in being
called to be a "tramp for the Lord" over the whole world.
"Une troubadoure de Dieu."

My sister Betsie, who was with me in the concentration
camp, had a vision. She awakened me in the middle of the

night to share it with me. "Corrie, God has spoken to me. When we are free, we must do two things. We must open a house for these prisoners around us. Those who come out alive will have a difficult time to find their way through life again. They are morally wounded. God will give us a beautiful big house, and many will be healed there. But we must not stay there. We must travel over the whole world. We have a message for the world. From experience we can now tell that a child of God can never go so deep into darkness that he will not always find beneath him the everlasting arms that uphold him."

A week later Betsie died. Shortly after that I was set free. I started the two things that God had shown to Betsie.

The house for ex-prisoners was opened in Bloemendaal less than a year after I came out of prison. It is now an international centre operated by the ten Boom Foundation as a home for those who need rest and relaxation. The war-weary people are back in their own homes again, and now many guests from Holland and from other lands spend their vacation in the beautiful house, "Zonneduin" ("Sunny Dune House").

In my book *Amazing Love* I cover some of my experiences travelling in many countries. In an earlier book, *A Prisoner and Yet* . . . I describe what happened to my life in underground work and in prison camps during the War.

In this third book I have included some things I have learned through meeting a great variety of people around the world, but more of the things He has taught me who said, "Lo, I am with you alway, even unto the end of the world."

Connected with Him in His love, I am more than conqueror; without Him, I am nothing. Like some railway tickets in America, I am "Not good if detached".

CHAPTER II

FIRST STEPS ON A WORLD TOUR

"Teach me Thy way, O Lord."—Psa. 27 : 11.

Now I am about to obey the second half of God's commission. He has told me to go to America, but I find
that many papers are needed. I must visit so many offices.
This is the first difficult test of obedience to the guidance
upon which I now depend. When my parents were married
they were given the verse, "I will instruct thee and teach
thee in the way which thou shalt go : I will guide thee with
Mine eye" (Psa. 32 : 8). This promise becomes my special
directive for all my journeyings.

Wherever I go, the answer is, "No papers are available
for America."

I pray, "Lord, if it is Your will that I go to America, they
must provide papers." Again and again God performs a
miracle. After some time I have most of the papers in my
hand.

Man's importunity is God's opportunity. He uses our
problems as building materials for His miracles. These are
my first steps on the path to complete dependence on and
obedience to His guidance. How much I still have to learn !

At last I have all my papers except one. The worst obstacle
seems to await me at the tenth office. Everyone coming out
warns those of us waiting in the hall, "That fellow in there
is as hard as flint; he passes no one." I have to wait a long
time.

Three ladies and a gentleman pass me. One of the ladies
stops. "Hello there ! Don't we know each other? Aren't you
a cousin of mine?" We have not seen each other for years.
She introduces her husband.

I ask, "Are you, too, planning to go to America?"

"Not at all. My office is in this building."

"Then perhaps you can help me," and I tell him my
story.

"I'm sorry; I'd like to be of service to my brand-new

cousin, but that's not in my department. However, if you have trouble, ring me up." And he gives me his office telephone number.

Time passes, and the "man of stone" goes out for coffee. A very young clerk takes his place. When my turn comes, he says, "You had better wait until my boss returns."

"No! I can't wait any longer. Won't you please call this number?"

I give him the telephone number of my cousin. The side of the conversation I hear is encouraging. Hanging up the telephone, he says, "Yes, you may have your papers." The miracle has happened. Now for ship reservations.

In Amsterdam I try to arrange my passage on a ship of the Holland–America line. I am told, "We'll put your name on the waiting list and call you when there is room. It may take ten or twelve months."

Surely that cannot be true! It has been made so plain to me that I must go *now*.

Disappointed, I stand in the Square and notice that the American Express Company has opened an office. I might try for a berth on a freighter. Stepping into the office, I inquire, "Have you passenger accommodation on freighters to America?"

"You may sail tomorrow, madam, if your papers are in order."

"But tomorrow is too sudden. What about next week?"

"That, too, can be arranged."

So I come to America. New York is a great city. The skyscrapers are so very tall, and Corrie ten Boom is so very small. Fifty dollars is all I have taken with me; more is not permitted. But there are two cheques in my pocket. While still in Holland I had told my plans to an American visiting relatives there. Shaking his head, he had warned me that it was not easy to make one's way in America.

"I believe you, but God has directed me and I must obey."

He had given me a large cheque and a smaller one. "If you need them, use them, and you can repay me later."

In New York a Y.W.C.A. provides me with a room for one week. I speak that week to several groups of Jewish Christian immigrants. Since they are German, I cannot use the English lectures I have prepared while on board ship.

When I pay the rent for my room at the end of the week the clerk asks where she should send my suit-cases.

"I am unable to say at present," I reply.

"I am so sorry, but our accommodation is so limited that we cannot allow you to stay here any longer."

"Yes, I know, but God has another room for me. It is just that I don't know the address."

She looks perplexed, but I am not worried. God led me through Ravensbrück! He will surely see me through America.

Then suddenly she recalls, "There is a letter for you."

How can that be, since nobody knows where I am staying? But there it is.

I read the letter, and say, "My suit-cases go to this address," and I give her the number of a house in 190th Street.

"But why didn't you tell me that before?"

"I didn't know. It's in this letter. A woman writes, 'I heard you speak this week to the Jewish congregation. I am aware that it is almost impossible to get a room in New York City. My son happens to be in Europe, so you are welcome to use his room as long as you are staying in New York.'"

The lady at the desk is more amazed than I am. Perhaps she has not experienced so many miracles as I have.

The subway takes me to 190th Street. It is a large house occupied by many families. At the end of a hall is the number I am looking for, but my hostess is away. She certainly could not have expected her invitation to be an eleventh-hour answer to my problem. Arranging myself among my suit-cases, I soon fall asleep, for I am tired. Thus she finds me when she returns after midnight; and I become her guest for five weeks.

Five weeks that test my faith. One cheque has already been cashed. Jan ten Have, the publisher of my books in Holland, is in New York. He is a faithful friend, and helps me as much as he can. My time is spent looking up addresses given me in Holland, and telling my experiences. The Americans are friendly and say my story is interesting. They will keep me in mind, but they are unable to arrange meet-

ings for me at present. However, they give me some more
names. I call on these also. Not all are polite. Some even
say I should have stayed in Holland.

"Why did you come to America?" so many ask.

"God has directed me and I can only obey," is my reply.

"That's nonsense. There is no such thing as direct guidance from God. Experience proves that you must use your
common sense."

"Sure I must use my common sense, but God's guidance
is even more important, and I am certain I have to bring a
message here. I can declare that the deepest darkness is out-
shone by the light of Jesus."

"We have our ministers to tell us such things."

"Certainly; but I can tell from my experiences in a concentration camp that what the ministers say is true."

"It would have been better for you to have remained in
Holland. Too many Europeans come to America. They
should be stopped."

Are they right? My money is all gone, except the larger
cheque. I do not want to cash it before seeing the man who
gave it to me. I find his address and arrive in an imposing
business office. His face is no longer so friendly.

"Do you mind if I cash your other cheque?" I ask.

"How do I know if or when you can return my money?
Have not five weeks in America been long enough to prove
there is no work here for you? Please return my cheque."

He writes me another bearing a much smaller amount.

Mustering all my courage, I say, "I am sure God has work
here for me. I am in His will, and will soon return your
money."

I am embarrassed and humbled. I have money in Holland : a balance left from my first book, and a small income
from the business I sold; but these funds cannot be brought
to America.

In my room I have a long consultation with my heavenly
Father, reciting all my troubles.

"Father, you must help me out," I pray. "If I must bor-
row money to return to Holland people will say, 'There, you
see, the promises of the Bible are not really meant. Direct
guidance does not exist.' Father, for Your own honour's
sake, You must help me out."

The answer is clear. "Do not worry about My honour. I will take care of that. In days to come you will give thanks for these days in New York."

A great burden is lifted from my soul.

When I awake the next day the thought that a great ocean separates me from my homeland oppresses me, as it has every morning since coming here. All the worries appear again. I have no money. Nobody wants to hear my message. Was it really God's guidance? Then comes the comforting assurance of last night. God has promised to take care of His honour, and in time I will be thankful for these days.

What a joy that God never leaves His children alone. He is a faithful guide for everyone who listens to His voice. "The Lord taketh pleasure in those that hope in His mercy" (Psa. 147 : 11).

That day a Dutch service is held in a New York church. Dr. Barkay Wolf speaks, and many Hollanders meet afterwards for coffee in the vestry. The Reverend Burggraaff, who baptised our Canadian-born princess, is presented to me. The name, ten Boom, revives a memory.

"I often tell the story of a nurse by that name," he says, "who experienced a miracle in a concentration camp with a bottle of vitamins. I tell it to prove that God still performs miracles as in Bible times. Do you happen to know that nurse? Is she related to you?"

"She is not a nurse," I reply, "but a watchmaker. It was I who had that experience in 1944."*

"Then you must come with me to Staten Island, and tell my congregation of your experiences."

Together we go to the pleasant parsonage, where I spend five delightful days with those happy Christians and their two sweet children.

Mrs. Burggraaff is an excellent cook. I have been trying to discover how long one can exist on Nedick's 10-cent breakfasts : a large cup of coffee, two doughnuts, and a glass of orange juice, eaten while standing at a counter. The delicious nourishing food is a joy, but the real reason for my happiness is that I have ended my lesson in obedience, and feel that God is at work opening doors and hearts.

* *A Prisoner and Yet . . .*, page 97.

Returning to New York, I see on a church door an invitation to attend the Lord's Supper. What a blessing lies in Holy Communion. As truly as I taste the bread and wine, the Lord's body was broken for me, and His blood shed for me. How I had missed the Sacrament while in prison. On Sunday morning I shall go to that church. It will be Easter Sunday.

The churches of America have a friendly welcome for strangers. The minister greets me and gives me the address of Irving Harris, the editor of *The Evangel*, a monthly magazine distributed throughout America and many other lands. The next day I am telling him about my problems.

"I know I am walking in the way God has led me, but so many declare that there is no such thing as direct guidance."

"Pay no attention to the counsel of those who do not believe in guidance," he answers. "The Bible contains many promises that God will lead those who obey Him. 'Call unto Me, and I will answer thee' (Jer. 33 : 3). Have you ever heard of a Good Shepherd that did not lead his sheep?"

I am content. I know he is right.

"Do you have any copy that would be useful for my magazine?" he asks.

I give him a copy of my lectures, and tell him to use as much as he can.

"There is one drawback," he explains. "We cannot pay. This paper exists only to spread the Gospel, not for financial profit."

Wonderful! I am in the presence of an American who sees money in its proper perspective. "Seek ye first the kingdom of God, and His righteousness; and all these things shall be added unto you" (Matt. 6 : 33).

Mr. Harris gives me an address in Washington. Does it mean I am being fobbed off again? No, I have found a true friend, and with this recommendation Abraham Vereide receives me as a friend into his home. He invites me to dinner. Three other guests are present, professors who ask difficult questions. I feel like a schoolgirl invited out by her headmistress. My English is not very fluent, and my mistakes seem more glaring than ever before. But I do my utmost to use my eyes and ears. I can learn much here listening to the conversation. I hear a good illustration. Mr.

Vereide speaks about our relationship with Jesus, and shows a train ticket. Printed on it are the words: "Not good if detached."

From now on I choose that phrase as my slogan. Connected with Jesus, His victory is my victory. "Not good if detached from Him."

That afternoon I am asked to address a group of women. Whenever I am asked to witness to what the Lord meant to me during my imprisonment I am in my element. I can tell that Jesus Christ is a reality, even in darkest days. He is the answer to all the problems in the hearts of men and nations. It is evident that the Holy Spirit is at work in this meeting. There is response from these women who gather once a week for prayer and Bible study.

That evening one of them gives me a cheque that enables me to return all the money I borrowed in New York.

Now the tables are turned. Instead of no work, I must guard against overwork. Ten months in America, in many villages and towns. Ten months of carrying the Gospel to churches, prisons, universities, schools, and clubs.

Then the pillar of fire and the cloud lead to Germany. The one land in the world where I do not want to go.*

F. B. Meyer says, "God does not fill with His Holy Spirit those who believe in the fulness of the Spirit, or those who desire Him, but those who obey Him."

When I left the German concentration camp I said, "I'll go anywhere God sends me, but I hope never to Germany." Though I was unaware of it, that was disobedience.

In America there comes a time when guidance no longer seems to be given. When I pray no answer comes. I realise that the trouble is not with the Good Shepherd, but with the sheep, and I ask, "Lord, am I disobeying you in some way?"

The answer comes clearly, "Germany."

A struggle follows, but victory soon comes, and I am able to say, "Yes, Lord, to Germany also."

* *Amazing Love*, page 27.

CHAPTER III

RETURN TO GERMANY

The time is short,
Too short toward any living
To cherish enmity.
Lay it aside
For His dear sake, forgiving
As He forgiveth thee.
Author unknown

AT a meeting in a friend's home I see a woman who does not look into my eyes. On asking my hostess who she is I am told that she is one of the nurses from the concentration camp, Ravensbrück. Suddenly I recognise her. Ten years ago I had to take my sister Betsie to the hospital barracks in the concentration camp where we were prisoners. Her feet were paralysed. She was dying. This nurse was cruel to her and scolded her. At that moment of recognition hatred comes into my heart. I thought I had overcome it, but now I see her again, after all these years, and great bitterness is in my heart. For ten years I have harboured this hatred. Oh, the shame of it!

When I bring my sins to the Lord Jesus He casts them into the depths of the sea—forgiven and forgotten. He also puts up a sign, "NO FISHING ALLOWED!"

And I? Ten years, and I have neither forgiven nor forgotten what this woman did.

Ashamed, I confess my guilt. "Forgive me for my hatred, O Lord. Teach me to love my enemies."

What a joy that there is forgiveness, and salvation from sin. The blood of Jesus Christ cleanses us from all sins if we confess them. It has never cleansed excuses. Instead of hatred, love enters my heart. After the meeting I try to speak with her, but she is unwilling to talk.

The next day I think of her, and pray for her. I believe in the power of praying together. Jesus has said, "Where two or three are gathered together in My name, there am I

in the midst of them." Not "I come", but "I am". Jesus is
there first. He invites the twos and threes to come. That is
why I ask my hostess if she will pray with me. Then she
tells me that a group of young girls have been praying for
the nurse and for her salvation for several months.

That gives me courage. When people pray for the salvation of someone it indicates that God is working. He puts it
in our hearts and minds to intercede; and what God begins,
He will complete.

I find the address of the hospital where the nurse works,
and call her by telephone. I tell her that I have a meeting
that night and would be very happy if she would come.

Amazed, she asks, "What? Do *you* want *me* to come?"

"Yes; that is why I called you."

"Then I'll come."

The whole evening she listens, and looks straight into my
eyes. I know that she listens with her heart. After the meeting I read with her from the Bible the way of salvation.
1 John 4 : 9 clinches the matter : "In this was manifested
the love of God toward us, because that God sent His only
begotten Son into the world, that we might live through
Him." She makes the decision that causes the angels to
rejoice. Not only has my hatred gone, but I can love her.
And I, who have kept in my subconsciousness feelings of
hatred, the Lord now uses as a window through which His
light can shine into her dark heart : His channel for streams
of living water. What miraculous power there is in the blood
of Jesus ! He forgives, cleanses, and then makes us His in-
strument. He cleanses the earthen vessel that contains the
treasure. Sinners, saved sinners, He uses as His ambassadors. What wonderful grace !

THE WRONG ADDRESS

A sick woman sits in a dirty, messy little kitchen. There
is hardly room for my stool. I am eager for a quiet talk with
her because she has twice called on a fortune-teller who
claimed magic healing power. I tell her what a great sin
this is in God's sight, because it really means that we run
away from God and ask the devil for help. That is why God
calls this sin an abomination (Deut. 18 : 10–12).

A great compassion comes into my heart for this woman.

I tell her about the longing father-heart of God who loves us so much and who brought us in contact with an ocean of love through Jesus Christ. That is why God thinks it so terrible when we seek help from the enemy.

I notice that she is now listening differently. When I warned her earnestly she defended herself and resisted. Now I tell her with joy about that great love of God. She listens intently. I read to her what Jesus says: "Come unto Me, all ye that labour and are heavy laden, and I will give you rest" (Matt. 11 : 28). Before I leave she prays. She asks forgiveness for going to the fortune-teller, and then she praises and thanks God for the great riches she has in Jesus Christ.

BATTLE AGAINST POWERS OF DARKNESS

In Germany many people turn to the sin of sorcery and witchcraft. Is this true in other lands, I wonder? Many who talk with me complain of a darkness in their hearts that cannot be lifted, or ever-recurring thoughts of suicide. When I ask if they have called upon a fortune-teller they reply that they have, but they do not really believe in her power.

In the days of uncertainty when Germans in captivity were unable to send messages home, wives and mothers yearned to know the fate of their loved ones. Many visited fortune-tellers. Whether or not they got answers I do not know, but it is evident that the powers of darkness entered their hearts. They do not seem to know that this is sin.

Whether this is done out of curiosity or "just for fun", it gives entrance to demonic powers. So whenever I have a full week of meetings, one evening is reserved for proving from the Bible the sin of this practice. The wearing of amulets and charms, and the foretelling of events by cards and horoscopes are all an abomination in God's sight. Deuteronomy 18 : 10–12 warns us, "There shall not be found among you any one that maketh his son or his daughter to pass through the fire, or that useth divination, or an observer of times, or an enchanter, or a witch, or a charmer, or a consulter with familiar spirits, or a wizard, or a necromancer. For all that do these things are an abomination unto the Lord : and because of these abominations the Lord thy God doth drive them out from before thee."

It is wonderful to have an answer also to this problem.

Jesus came to overcome the works of Satan. The Bible says, "They overcame him [Satan] by the blood of the Lamb, and by the word of their testimony" (Rev. 12:11). Ours is the victory through the blood of the Lamb and the testimony of our witness.

Those that are with us are greater than those that are against us. We need not remain in the dark. Jesus said, "I am the Light of the world : he that followeth Me shall not walk in darkness, but shall have the light of life" (John 8:12). We possess the authority of His name.

How great a joy it is to bring the Good News of Jesus' victory into this darkness. But whenever I give this message I am so tired I can hardly reach my bed. My heart beats irregularly, and I feel that I am not at all well.

One evening I have a long talk with my heavenly Father. "I cannot continue like this, dear Lord. Why must I testify against this particular sin? So many of your faithful servants never mention it. I can't go on like this much longer, and live. Perhaps another month or two, and then my heart will give out."

Then in the *Losungsbuch*, a book of daily readings in German, I read, "Be not afraid, but speak, and hold not thy peace : for I am with thee, and no man shall set on thee to hurt thee" (Acts 18 : 9, 10). A short poem follows :

> Though all the powers of hell attack,
> Fear not, Jesus is Victor.

Joy fills my heart; this is God's answer. I pray, "Lord, I will obey, I will not fear and be silent. But with my hands on this promise I ask You to protect me with Your blood, that the demons cannot touch me."

At that moment something happens to my heart; it beats regularly. I know I am healed. After this when having spoken against sorcery and witchcraft, I feel as well as ever before. Jesus is Victor! The fear of demons comes from the demons themselves. We have nothing to be afraid of. Those who are with us are greater than those who are against us. Hidden with Christ in God : what a refuge! The mighty High Priest and His legions of angels are on our side.

RESIST THE DEVIL—OURS IS THE VICTORY

In a small town in Germany a group of students plan a week-end. Ten Christians have each brought an outsider. Though the only speaker, I feel we are a team, these ten and I. There is much prayer and discussion between meetings, and when Sunday evening comes eight students have accepted Jesus as their personal Saviour.

Trudy, a medical student, follows me that evening as, tired but grateful, I go to my room. "Corrie, thank you so much for all you have done for Heinz. He is my fiancé, and he is so different today. Before he was all gloom; now he is truly happy."

"What a joy, Trudy. Let us thank the Lord, for He has done it. I am only a branch of the Vine, a channel for His blessing. But tell me, Trudy, what about yourself?"

"I haven't come to speak about myself; I wish only to speak of Heinz."

"All right. Then we speak about the change in Heinz, who has come out of darkness into God's marvellous light."

Suddenly I turn to Trudy and address the demons within her. In Jesus' name I bid them leave and go back to hell, where they belong. I see immediately a great change in Trudy's face. Astounded, she asks, "Is there hope for me?" Then she falls to her knees and cries, "I am free; thank You, Lord, I am free!"

With deep joy Trudy praises the Lord, then confesses she contemplated committing suicide the next day. Looking into her eyes, I see she is not entirely free, but she leaves my room praising the Lord. My legs are trembling. I had known nothing about the girl, and all this seems to have happened outside of myself. What a victory! Though it is late, I go downstairs to find someone to join me in prayer. In the meeting-room I find all the students on their knees.

"I've come to tell you that Trudy is free."

"Yes, we know."

"What do you know? Who told you?"

"We know she was under the influence of demons. When we saw her go to your room we all knelt in prayer and asked God to use you to deliver her. Suddenly our prayer became praise, and we knew she was free."

"She is not entirely free. Keep on praying for her until she is completely liberated."

Three days later I speak at the University which Trudy attends, but she hides behind others. The boys ask me to speak to her, but I have no guidance. A week later she looks me up in a town where I am working, and God uses me to finish the work He began in her.

I am well aware I do not possess the special gift to cast out demons, but in times of emergency we must dare to lay hold on the promise of Mark 16 : 17, "In My name shall they cast out devils."

MORE THAN PSYCHOLOGY

Psychology is profitable, even necessary, but not enough. I recall a conversation with a German pastor. It had been a busy and difficult counselling session. Six people had complained about great inner darkness and thoughts of suicide. Some I had been able to help, but not all.

"Can't you help me?" I asked the pastor. "In cases like these working together is so much better. One can pray while the other casts out demons."

The pastor answered me with a discourse on the defence-mechanism of the subconscious. That was no help to me. How dangerous to try to solve great problems with small answers.

A theological professor was asked, "Do you teach your students to cast out demons?"

"Hardly," was the answer. "I can't do that myself."

"But you dare to send students to congregations that are filled with sorcery? Do you think their knowledge of the Jahist and the Elohist manuscripts of Genesis will help them when they are struggling with the demons that have entered so many people of our day?"

> Soldiers of Christ, arise,
> And put your armour on,
> Strong in the strength which God supplies
> Through His eternal Son;
> Strong in the Lord of hosts,
> And in His mighty power,
> Who in the strength of Jesus trusts
> Is more than conqueror.

Leave no unguarded place,
No weakness of the soul;
Take every virtue, every grace,
And fortify the whole.
From strength to strength go on,
Wrestle and fight and pray,
Tread all the powers of darkness down
And win the well-fought day.

Charles Wesley.

GOD'S LOVE NEVER FAILS

Once Betsie, my sister, and I walked through the colourless streets of a concentration camp.

"Corrie, these barracks here are used to destroy lives. We must pray God to give us such a camp after the war to build up lives."

What fantasy to see such possibilities in so terrible a place! No, it was not fantasy : it was faith. Faith sees the invisible, just as the radar of a ship throws its beam straight through the fog to the other ships. So faith shows God's love and Jesus' victory, even through the chaos of our life.

Many years later I walk again through the streets of a concentration camp. The war is over, but left behind are many wounds for many nations; perhaps the most serious wounds in Germany itself. In many countries there are refugees, homeless people, but here the problem seems almost beyond solution. No use trying to solve it—but no, we must not say that. Everyone must do what he can. God gave me a concentration camp. It was in Darmstadt, where shortly after the War I found several of my former guards. They were then prisoners; I was free. They had been very cruel. How their experiences during the War had demoralised them. Young women still, now imprisoned behind barbed wire; but more imprisoned by demoniacal powers. I could speak to them of Jesus' victory, His love for sinners and His finished work on the Cross when He carried the sins of the whole world, theirs included.

When I returned to the camp it was empty. The women had been freed or sent to other prisons. The same week I rented the whole camp, and now it is a place where refugees can stay while they build houses in the neighbourhood.*

* See *Amazing Love*, page 34.

When in Germany I visit the camp. I look around me.
The barracks are grey, the streets between colourless. I tell
Walter Zipf, the director, that it still looks like a prison
camp. We make plans, and that very week God gives me
enough money to enable us to fulfil them.

What a change bright-green paint and flowers, many
flowers, can make to a place! Two months later I receive a
coloured photograph, and now, with a little bit of imagina-
tion, it is more like a Hollywood home than a prison camp.

Human love has failed in this world, but the love of God
is shed abroad in our hearts by the Holy Spirit who is given
to us (Rom. 5 : 5). It is this love that overcomes, and is able
to change even a colourless prison camp into a garden of
flowers.

A MINISTERS' MEETING

Working in Germany is a delight. The ministers and I
get along well, working, praying and striving together. A
team travelling with me would be ideal, but since that is not
yet possible, God has given me as team-mates the ministers
in whose churches I work. Though differing in background
and training, our common aim unites us : the winning of
souls for eternity, and helping the children of God to learn
that "Jesus is Victor".

Speaking at a ministers' meeting is another story.
Frequently it is among them that I find my severest critics,
and sometimes even my greatest opposition. Yet it seems
vital to be used of God among them, for these men who work
in over-large congregations and are weighed down with
problems also need to be reminded of Jesus' victory and His
plan for the world.

A large group waits for me to speak. Shall I try to convince them *not* to listen to me but to God and His message
for us?

"Gentlemen, I am a lay person, a lay woman, a Dutch
lay woman. Are there some present who would rather not
remain?

"I intend to speak about conversion. Perhaps you have a
label for me . . . a Pietist? I shall speak about the Lord's
return : that should label me a Sectarian. I may even speak
about the rapture of the Church : that makes me a Fanatic;

or the fulness of the Holy Spirit : a Pentecostal. Keep your labels handy, gentlemen. Should my words touch your consciences, you have only to label me, set me in a corner and have nothing to fear."

A strange thing happens. The critical faces relax. There is laughter, after which we truly listen together to God's message : Germany's great need, and Christ the answer to this need. The world's history is a great embroidery by God, enough of which is made clear to us through His Word so that we can face the future calm and secure, since all is in His hand. Indeed, the best is yet to be—a world full of the knowledge of the Lord, as the waters cover the sea.

When I finish, with one accord the group turns to prayer.

CARL

"Behold I saw an ocean of light and love flow over an ocean of darkness and death, and in that I saw the infinite love of God, and the day it flowed over the ocean of darkness and death was when Jesus said, 'It is finished!' " (Wesley).

Everywhere in Germany I find the wounds and scars of war. I read a letter a mother has received from her son, Carl, now a prisoner in the Netherlands. He was a prison guard during the War, and has been sentenced to sixteen years' imprisonment in the very jail where he had practised his cruelties. He writes, "Father, Mother, I have accepted the Lord Jesus as my Saviour. He has made me a child of God. I have brought all my sins to Him and He has cast them into the depths of the sea."

After reading that letter I decide to request an amnesty for him from my Queen. A child of God has power in his struggle against Satan. He has the authority of Jesus' name. Even as a traffic policeman is backed by the authority of the law, and traffic stops at his signal, so too, Satan has to yield to the name of Jesus. Every child of God can wield the authority of the Name that is above every other name. That is why I can trust Carl.

Before I write the letter to the Queen I decide to go to Vught to call on Carl. Again I see that courtyard where Betsie and I stood, not knowing what was in store for us. We stood between rows of men who told us we might well be shot. I tremble as I see this spot once more. Then I enter the cell occupied by Carl, my former prison guard.

"I come to bring you greetings from your parents, Carl."

"Do you mean to say you have seen them?"

"Certainly; I've just returned from Germany."

Carl's eyes fill with tears, and he whispers, "How is Mother?"

"She's well, Carl, and so happy you have decided for Jesus and are now a child of God." I describe my visit to his parents and friends, and then add, "I, too, was in prison here."

"You were? When?"

"In 1944."

Carl's face turns pale. "Then we know each other."

"Yes, we know each other."

In memory we both recall Carl's cruelties of those days, but a joyful look lights his face as he says, "How happy I am that my sins have been taken away."

I say nothing, but a dark thought wells up in my soul : Is it as easy as that? Due to your barbarism and the cruelties of others, my father, Betsie, Kik, my cousin, and many of my friends perished in prisons and concentration camps. But you are no longer guilty!

It is an immutable law of God that man finds peace only when he is continually ready to forgive. Suddenly I see what I am doing. Carl's sins have been cast by Jesus into the depths of the sea. They are forgiven and forgotten—and I am trying to fish them up again! I pray, "Father, in Jesus' name forgive these thoughts. Lord Jesus, keep me close to You as the branch is close to the vine, that I may be able to forgive and forget, and love my enemies."

Only now do I trust myself to speak again. "Indeed, Carl, your sins have been taken away. Our Lord has taken upon Himself the sins of the whole world, including yours and mine. I have something more to tell you. I am planning to write to the Queen to ask an amnesty for you."

A lesson is learned there in Carl's cell. When Jesus requires that we love our enemies, He gives us the love He demands from us. We are channels of His love, not reservoirs. Truly, if I had been a reservoir, at that moment it would have sprung a great leak and all the love would have drained away. Again my American railway ticket gives the answer, "Not good if detached." That is me! I have been detached. But when I am united with Him who prayed on the cross, "Father, forgive them; for they know not what they do", I can forgive and forget, and even love my enemies. Without Him I am embittered and am prone to hate. Therefore I want ever to remain close to Him, as the branch is to the Vine, "That My joy might remain in you, and that your joy might be full" (John 15:11). Once we learn to love our enemies we tap the ocean of God's love as never before.

CHAPTER IV

STORM

"As the branch cannot bear fruit of itself, except it abide in the vine; no more can ye, except ye abide in Me."—(John 15 : 4.)

IT is so tiring to hold the edge of my bed during the rolling of the ship that I fasten myself with a rope to my mattress. I am the only passenger on board the freighter, and I must share my cabin with the gyrocompass. I am a bad sailor and find sea travel a tribulation. Suddenly a huge wave hurls against the ship and I hear a strange sound. The gyrocompass whistles night and day, but now it is broken and the noise is peculiar. One of the engineers comes to repair it.

"Is this a bad storm?" I ask.

"Why, no! This is nothing at all. Wait until the wind force is 14, then we shall really know what rolling is."

At that moment, as if to contradict his words, a big wave throws the ship to one side. I hear the breaking of china, and everything that is not securely fastened runs from one side of the cabin to the other.

The storm has subsided by next morning, so I climb up to the bridge and meet the captain. After a chat about the weather, I say, "Captain, it is Sunday. May we have a church service?"

"What? A church service on my ship? It would be the first in my life!"

"Then," I reply with a smile, "it is high time you began, sir."

"All right. You can use the mess-room. I am not opposed to the idea."

He himself writes on the notice-board that at 11 a.m. there will be a church service in the mess-room. At the appointed time nobody appears. The cabin boy brings me a cup of coffee. It is a Dutch ship, and the ship's cook knows that at 11 a.m. a cup of coffee is a tradition.

"Are you going to stay?" I asked the boy. "I have a very interesting story to tell you."

"I don't want to hear that nonsense," he says. "I will not have anything to do with that Bible and God business." He feels very cocksure, and leaves me alone.

I never saw so empty a church; just a cup of coffee and myself. I am not at all on fire for the Lord. Were I enthusiastic, I would go to the bridge and say, "Come along, gentlemen; you must help me to fill the mess-room. Send your men and boys." But I don't do that. I go to my cabin and am very seasick. That is the only thing I can do during the whole week.

Sunday comes round again. I am feeling discouraged and ashamed. "Lord, I have now been on this ship for almost ten days, and I have done nothing to bring the Gospel to all these men who may lose their souls for eternity. Lord, I am not a missionary. Send me back to my watchmaking business. I am not worthy to do your work."

At that moment I find in my Bible a little piece of paper which I have never seen before. On it is written :

> Cowardly, wayward, and weak,
> I change with the changing sky,
> Today so eager and strong,
> Tomorrow not caring to try.
> But He never gives in,
> And we two shall win,
> > Jesus and I.

Instantly I see it! Indeed I am not worthy at all. The branch without the Vine cannot produce fruit, but I can do all things through Christ who gives me strength. The strongest and the weakest branches are worth nothing without the Vine; but connected to it they have the same nature.

I go up to the bridge. "Captain, it is Sunday. Can we have a church service?"

"Again? In a church as empty as last week?" he asks teasingly.

"No, Captain. Not empty, but full, and you must help me."

He does, and there are ten men in the mess-room. When my sermon is finished the cabin boy says, "It was not boring at all!"

CHAPTER V

AMBASSADORS FOR CHRIST

Make me a match that can kindle a fire.

BERMUDA, island of wealth and bright colours, deep-blue sea, white-walled houses, and an abundance of flowers.

Bermuda, land of ever-smiling sunshine.

But Bermuda also has prisons. I speak in one soon after my arrival. While I tell of God's great love in Jesus Christ, and the riches which abide in any circumstance if we "cash our cheques", that is, act on His Word, God touches the heart of the prison director.

"Please come again," he says. "You speak a language the prisoners understand."

I am eager to return. "How often may I come?"

"As often as you wish."

"Twice a day?" When I am offered a finger I take the whole hand. Such opportunities are rare. Usually one chance to speak is all that is permitted in prisons. Then one often leaves with a heavy heart. How one would like to delve deeper into the prisoner's problems, and draw more generously from the bottomless ocean of the riches of Christ's love.

But here this splendid offer, "Agreed; twice a day."

Arrangements are made for a meeting with the assembled prisoners each morning, and an hour is spent in the evening going from cell to cell. Cell doors are barred with heavy iron grills. Standing outside, I read the Scriptures to the inmates. The attendant, a Negro of great understanding, takes me to a man who desperately needs an encouraging word, or to another who has requested an interview. He shows much tact, for he withdraws and remains at a distance till I give a sign that I am ready to go.

In one cell there are two Negroes. One keeps himself in the background while the other tells me his troubles, his hands tensed around the bars of his cell. What a joy! How glorious that with the utmost conviction I can tell him that the Lord Jesus carried the sins of the whole world; that He finished this task for him, too. From my spiritual "first-aid kit" I read some verses to show the way of salvation. Witnessing and telling of my own experiences may be important, but the Word of God is the "sharp two-edged sword".

Even while speaking I am in constant prayer. Both the vertical and the horizontal contacts are necessary. After all, it is not I who am at work, but the Holy Spirit working through me as a channel, a branch of the Vine. I pray that God may remove all the man's "ifs" and "buts" that the way from darkness to God's marvellous light may be opened. Finally, he says, "Yes, Lord Jesus."

Nothing more? No, not yet. But it means that he has accepted the Lord as his Saviour and is now a child of God (John 1 : 12); that he has opened the door of his heart to Him who stands outside and knocks, and now promises to come and abide with him (Rev. 3 : 20).

"Do you know how to pray?" I ask the Negro crouched in a corner of the cell.

"Oh, yes."

"Then please come here."

He comes, and I ask him to clasp the hand of his cellmate while I take his other hand and the hand of the man who has just decided for Jesus. A tiny prayer-circle reaching through the bars of a prison door.

"Will you pray first?"

"Our Father which art in heaven, Hallowed be Thy name . . ."

Suddenly silence descends upon the corridor as the other Negro prisoners standing behind their doors hear one of their number pray.

"Thy kingdom come. Thy will be done on earth, as it is in heaven."

Are the others praying with us? Are their minds on that future when God's will shall be done on earth as it is in heaven? No more prisons there. The earth full of the knowledge of the Lord as the waters cover the sea.

"Give us this day our daily bread, and forgive us our trespasses, as we forgive them that trespass against us."

Forgiveness—no longer guilty, but mercifully pardoned.

"And lead us not into temptation, but deliver us from evil." The possibility of victory in the midst of evil.

"For Thine is the kingdom, and the power, and the glory, for ever and ever, Amen."

Prisoners speak to a King! Weak ones, poor ones. praying and giving thanks for power and glory. It is a sacred moment in the Bermuda prison. Have the demons left because angels are present? Jesus Himself is present. "Where two or three are gathered together in My name, there am I in the midst of them," He has said. There is joy among the angels over one sinner that is saved.

The sinner himself now prays. It is a poor little prayer; his first. Though stammering and stumbling, it is the thanks of one who for the first time has seen the marvellous light of God's love in Jesus Christ. It means, "Thank You, Lord Jesus, because You have saved me and will keep on saving me." Do I see tears in the eyes of the attendant as he takes me to another corridor?

In a cell corner I see a crouching figure, a red patch on the back of his prison uniform.

"Has he tried to escape?" I ask the attendant.

"Yes, but how did you know?"

"We also had to wear red patches if we tried to escape from prison."

"This is a tragic case. The man, a murderer, was sentenced to be flogged. He feared the beating so much that he tried to run away. Now he has had to bear double punishment."

Poor man! I pray, "Lord, help me to find the way to reach this man's heart."

Suddenly my own prison experiences come to my mind. When our fellow-prisoners were tortured we urged them to tell us all that had happened. It was hard listening, but it helped them to throw off their terrible experience. If it is possible to get this man to talk, perhaps I can find the way to his heart.

"Hello! Did you have a beating?" I ask.

"Yes."

"Was it bad?"

"Yes."

"Come, tell me. Did they take you to the hospital afterwards?"

"No, it wasn't that bad." He comes to the barred door and looks at me with wondering eyes. What kind of a woman is this who asks such questions?

And my heart says, "Thank you, God; he is already at the door!"

"Didn't they do anything for you?"

"Yes, they rubbed me with salve."

Then I inquire, "Is there hate in your heart?"

"Hate! I am full of hate."

"That is something I can understand."

"*You . . .?*"

"Certainly. I know how you feel." Then I tell him of the beatings I had in Ravensbrück and, even worse, the beatings given to my poor weak sister Betsie because she no longer had the strength to shovel dirt. Then hatred tried to enter into my heart, but a miracle happened, for Jesus filled my heart with God's love, and there was no room for hatred.

Then I say, "If you will accept Him as your Saviour, He will do the same for you."

I take my Bible and read, " 'As many as received Him, to them gave He power to become the sons of God' (John 1 : 12). Jesus is knocking at the door of your heart. If you will let Him, He will come in (Rev. 3 : 20)."

It is a struggle between life and death, but life wins. He, too, utters his "Yes" to Jesus, and the angels in Heaven rejoice. We pray together, and he also offers a stammering prayer. Then we shake hands through the bars.

"Ah, miss, just a moment. Have you a little more time?"

"Certainly. Why?"

"Across the hall in the third cell is a man in real trouble. Won't you tell him this same story of Jesus?"

A babe in Christ, not more than five minutes saved, and already he has a burden for souls. Only just saved himself, and he longs to share his joy with others.

So often people say, "I don't know enough myself. I'm too young in the faith to point out the way to others." Then I always ask, "How old a babe in Christ was the Samaritan woman when she declared to the entire city, 'Come, see a man, which told me all things that ever I did: is not this the Christ?'" Many went to Jesus, and later said to her, "Now we believe, not because of thy saying: for we have heard Him ourselves." A babe in Christ for only half an hour and already a wholesale soul winner!

I go to the cell across the hall, and have a long talk with the inmate. At last he understands what Jesus meant when He said, "Him that cometh to Me I will in no wise cast out." And he, too, accepts the Lord Jesus.

Before I leave the prison I go back to the murderer and tell him, "That was a wonderful thing you did when you sent me to the man across the hall. He, too, made a decision for Jesus." Then the Negro looks past me and cries, "Hi, brother!"

I think in that moment of a little poem:

> When I enter that beautiful city,
> And the saved all around me appear,
> I hope that someone will tell me,
> "It was you who invited me here."

What a joy when we reach Heaven to hear someone say, "Hi, brother! Hi, sister! You invited me here." Then indeed we shall know we have not lived in vain. Not hay, not stubble, but silver and gold have we built on the one foundation, Jesus Christ (1 Cor. 3:10–16).

Sometimes I am asked, "Can people really be saved so quickly?"

I always answer, "How long did it take Levi, the tax collector? Jesus said, 'Follow me', and he promptly closed his office and followed the Lord."

"Yes, but that was Jesus."

"Who do you suppose it was in the Bermuda prison? Do you think it was Corrie ten Boom who converted that man? No, it was Jesus who has said, 'Verily, verily, I say unto you, He that believeth on Me, the works that I do shall he do also; and greater works than these shall he do; because I go unto My Father'" (John 14:12).

Jesus is at the right hand of God the Father and does even greater things than He did during the three and a half years He taught in Palestine. But He works through His Church, you and me and all those who are united with Him, the branches of the Vine which bring forth good fruit.

"God, who first ordered light to shine in darkness has flooded our hearts with His light. We now can enlighten men only because we can give them knowledge of the glory of God, as we see it in the face of Jesus Christ. This priceless treasure we hold, so to speak, in a common earthenware jar—to show that the splendid power of it belongs to God and not to us" (2 Cor. 4 : 6, 7, Phillips). Streams of living water shall flow from us if we go through life united with Him.

CHAPTER VI

LONELINESS

God has plans—no problems. There is no panic in heaven.—Ian Thomas

LIVING in an isolated house in Canada is a woman who needs my help. It takes me a couple of hours to get there. When I arrive she is sitting in her chair, one arm on the table. She stares through the window at the wide prairie, which seems to be endless. Conversation is difficult, and during the moments when we are not talking the depressing silence in and around the house bears in on me.

I open the Bible and begin to read, " 'Yea, though I walk through the valley of the shadow of death, I will fear no evil : for Thou art with me" (Psa. 23 : 4). "Who shall separate us from the love of Christ? Shall tribulation, or depression, or loneliness? No, in all these things we are more than conquerors through Him that loved us' " (Rom. 8 : 35).

Then she begins to talk; at first slowly and hesitantly—then with greater confidence she describes the big city in Europe where she grew up. Then her marriage and subsequent emigration with her husband to Canada.

"I have five children. One of them is married; the others all work here on the ranch. They will come back tonight at six o'clock, and supper must be ready for them. When they are all at home it is not quiet here any more. At first we had our own farm where it was never quiet, for everyone in the family was always working in and around the house. But now they work for other farmers. We have had difficulties and setbacks—storms, drought, cattle sickness, and locusts. Then we came here, where it is so quiet and lonely."

When she finishes speaking she seems to be a little less unhappy. I can pray with her, and I know that she listens. Does she pray? When I get up to go she comes with me to the door. From the car, as I drive off, I can see her standing there. Is it the setting sun that brings a little colour to her cheeks? She waves to me and calls out, "Thank you." Will I ever hear of her again?

Yes, I do hear of her. A letter comes when I am alone in my cheerless hotel room in the big city. My windows look on to a small inner square; there is no sun, and almost no light. I open the letter. "Corrie, the evening after your visit, the woman killed her daughter with a gun. She is now in an asylum."

Is the devil victor? Poor woman. Poor family.

A great darkness enters my heart. What suffering there is in the world. This is only a drop in the ocean of misery on this earth. Have I failed? Have I done wrong? I do not often weep, but now I cannot restrain the tears. Then I take the Book that always gives comfort. "Cast thy burden upon the Lord." Yes, I need not carry it myself. He has carried our sorrows. I unpack my mental suit-case in prayer, and pray for grace to travel farther with it empty, and to leave my sorrows with Him. Then I read farther, "Behold, I make all things new," says Jesus (Rev. 21 : 5). "The earth shall be full of the knowledge of the Lord" (Isa. 11 : 9). "God shall wipe away all tears from their eyes" (Rev. 21 : 4).

I pray, "Lord Jesus, come quickly. It is so dark in the world." Then I read the psalms written by people in darkness and in the depths of misery, but who had found the answer by God's Spirit. "Hide not Thy face far from me . . . Thou hast been my help; leave me not, neither forsake me, O God of my salvation. . . . Wait on the Lord : be of good courage, and He shall strengthen thine heart : wait, I say, on the Lord" (Psa. 27 : 9, 14).

I do not understand it yet, but trustingly I put my hand in His hand, like a sad child who knows his father does not make mistakes.

I read another letter. A friend writes, "In Mexico, an automobile accident occurred. A missionary with four of his children and seven promising students of a Bible School were killed."

In Mexico, where the fields are already white unto harvest, and the labourers are few. What is the reason for it, Lord? I do not understand it. There seems no answer at all. One day we will understand. "At present all we see is the baffling reflection of reality; we are like men looking at a landscape in a small mirror. The time will come when we shall see reality whole and face to face! At present all I know is a little fraction of the truth, but the time will come when I shall know it as fully as God now knows me" (1 Cor. 13 : 12, Phillips).

CHAPTER VII

THE YOUNG CANADIAN

When Satan tempts me to despair
And tells me of my sins within;
Upwards I look and see Him there
Who made an end of all my sin.

I LIKE the Canadians. Is it because they combine, more o
less, that young, free attitude of the Americans with the
traditions of Britain? In Victoria I have a talk with a business-man. In his beautiful car he takes me to a church
where I am to speak that evening.

"Can you drive and pray at the same time?" I ask.

"Oh, yes. But we have time to park for five minutes. It is
a good thing to pray before going to church."

After we have prayed, he leans against his steering wheel
and tells me about himself.

"Years ago I accepted Jesus Christ as my Saviour. I have
read many books. I have studied my Bible during my quiet
time, and have listened to the best sermons it is possible to
hear in Victoria. But there is absolutely no joy in me. Sometimes I try to help people, but very soon pass them on to
others. In my heart there is bitterness instead of love. There
is . . ."

"You remind me of a branch of the vine which says, 'I
cannot understand why I bear no fruit.' It doesn't see that
the whole question is whether or not it is in contact with the
vine. Why not stop thinking of the fruit for a time, and
think only of the vine? Why have you no connection with
the Lord Jesus?"

"My sins. I am bitter, selfish, and unkind. What can you
do with your sins?"

"I always do what is written in 1 John 1 : 9 : confess my
sins."

"But it doesn't help. I remain bitter and dark."

"Do you believe that the blood of Jesus cleanses from
sins?"

"Sure I do."

"Where are the sins that you have confessed? What does the Bible say? Your bitterness is in the depths of the sea, forgiven and forgotten, and there is a little notice which says 'NO FISHING ALLOWED'. Your selfishness disappeared like that cloud we saw five minutes ago in the sky. Your unkindness is as far away from you as the east is from the west."

"But in a few minutes I am committing the same sins."

"When it is three o'clock and you are conscious of bitterness, confess it at three o'clock. You have an advocate with the Father—Jesus. He takes that sin on His own shoulders, and cleanses you with His blood. When the devil comes three minutes later to accuse you, there is no bitterness left. Be sure that you come to the Father with your sin three minutes sooner than the accuser. You can then say, with your hand on the Bible, 'God hath made Him to be sin for us, who knew no sin; that we might be made the righteousness of God in Him (2 Cor. 5 : 21). When Jesus died on the Cross He identified Himself with our death, and now you and I must identify ourselves with His life. So if the connection between the branch and the vine remains, the fruit comes from the vine. The branch does not help the vine. The vine does not help the branch. The vine does everything, and the branch must keep connected with it. That electric lamp there does not help the generator. The generator does not help the lamp. The generator gives all the power. The lamp must only be connected. You do not help the Holy Spirit. The Holy Spirit does not help you. The Holy Spirit does everything—the only condition is that you must keep in contact.

"It is such a joy to live by faith, simply acting on what the Bible says. Then Jesus' hand keeps hold of ours. Thank Him for that. In 1 Corinthians 15 : 57 it says, 'Thanks be to God, which giveth us the victory through our Lord Jesus Christ.'

"When the devil makes me depressed I always think of the immigrant and the peanuts. An immigrant and his family were on a big steamer. He had a bag full of peanuts, and at every meal-time they all ate peanuts. Of course, this diet became very monotonous, and one day the immigrant asked the purser how much it would cost for his family and himself to have one of the meals which he could smell cooking so deliciously. The purser answered smilingly that they were permitted to enjoy every meal served, without cost, as they had already been paid for when the immigrant tendered his passage money. Don't you think that the man changed his diet from the peanuts to the good meals which were served on the big steamer?

"Jesus paid for everything when He died on the cross. The handwriting of our sins is nailed on that cross. Turn away from your peanuts. Stop trying yourself, and take the riches that are yours through Jesus Christ. You are what you are in Him. Live like a king's child, and not like a beggar. Norman Grubb says: 'Break through the bands of HAVE-NOT-LIFE.' When all demons and men tell me 'You have not', then I declare, 'I have' because it is written.

"But don't forget to make right the wrong you have done. After you have asked forgiveness for unkindness, and you do not make it right with the person who has suffered through it, then you leave tools in the hands of the enemy. This restitution is given also through a branch connected with the vine. A child of God connected with Jesus Christ is right with God, and right with men.

"After you have confessed your sins, claim the promise Jesus made about the Holy Spirit, 'I will send Him unto you' (John 16 : 7). The Holy Spirit is here : Jesus sent Him at Pentecost. Obey the joyful commandment, 'Be filled with the Spirit' (Eph. 5 :18), and then the fruit will come.

"What fruit does the Holy Spirit have? He has love, joy, peace, longsuffering, gentleness, goodness, faithfulness, meekness, and self-control. Jesus was all these when He was on earth. I once read somewhere : 'The fruit of the Spirit is a perfect portraiture of Christ.'

"Love is the love of Christ that passes knowledge. Joy is the joy unspeakable and full of glory. Peace is the peace that passes all understanding that Jesus promised when He said, 'My peace I give unto you.' Longsuffering is forgiving—even your enemies, just as Jesus forgave His when He was on the cross. Gentleness is the reproduction of the gentleness of Jesus. Goodness is Christ-likeness : a kindly disposition. The next fruit is faithfulness. The disciples were not always faithful. At the betrayal of Jesus in the garden, they all forsook Him and fled. But when the Holy Spirit came down at Pentecost they all became faithful unto death. Meekness—that is not the same as weakness. Nor is it a native fruit of the human heart. It is an exotic from heaven. Self-control means mastering the appetites and passions, particularly the sensual.

"All this fruit can be seen in you, but only when you are in contact with the vine. You are 'not good if detached'."

Although I have a different sermon prepared, I speak that evening about the vine and the branch.

CHAPTER VIII

MEMORIES FROM A
CONCENTRATION CAMP

Faith in Jesus Christ makes the uplook good, the outlook high, the inlook favourable, and the future glorious.

IN thought I return to the years of my imprisonment. Because my friends and my family and I had housed and hidden Jews during the Nazi occupation we had been sent to the concentration camp in Ravensbrück. Fourteen hundred of us were packed in barracks built to house four hundred. It was unspeakably filthy. The vile blankets and thin mattresses on which we spent our days and nights were hosts to multitudes of vermin. Lice carried disease, rampant everywhere. But they performed one service for us; the "Aufseherinnen" (women guards) and officers never honoured the barracks with their presence. They had a healthy fear of our bugs. Therefore, though the Bible was strictly forbidden and dubbed a "Book of Lies", we could hold Bible studies twice a day in our barracks. God can use even vermin for His purposes.

Prisoners came to us from all directions and listened while we read and interpreted the Bible. Above and all around us, beds were closely stacked in triple tiers. There was respectful silence, and I know many were hearing the Good News of God's great love through Jesus Christ for the first time in their lives.

A Hollander, Mrs. De Boer, approached me one evening. She seemed desperate, her eyes full of fear. "Corrie, can you help me? I am afraid. I've just seen a woman cruelly beaten to death. It was terrible! When will my time come to be killed? I am afraid of death. Do help me. Perhaps you can tell me something from your Book that will take away this terrible fear."

"Yes, indeed I can," I replied. "This Book has the answer in John 1:12, 'As many as received Him, to them gave He power to become the sons of God.' If you are a child of God you need not fear death, for in John 14 we read, 'In My Father's house are many mansions!' 'I', Jesus said, 'go to prepare a place for you.' Children of God are at home in the Father's house. To them death is the gateway to heaven."

"That says nothing to me," answered Mrs. De Boer. "I'm not religious; I've never read the Bible; I don't attend church. When you say I must accept Jesus I simply don't know what you mean."

I prayed for wisdom. How can this mystery be made clear? How wonderful that we read in James 1 : 5 (Phillips), "If any of you does not know how to meet any particular problem he has only to ask God—who gives generously to all men without making them feel foolish or guilty—and he may be quite sure that the necessary wisdom will be given him."

"Do you recall years ago when Mr. De Boer proposed to you? How did you answer him?"

She smiled sadly and replied, "I said, 'Yes.' "

"Exactly. And when you had spoken that one little word you belonged to one another, you to him and he to you. Today Jesus asks, 'Will you accept Me as your Saviour?' If you say, 'Yes, Lord', then you belong to Him and He belongs to you."

"Is it as simple as that?" she asked.

"Yes. To become a child of God you need only to accept Him; salvation is a gift. Jesus says in Revelation 3 : 20, 'Behold, I stand at the door, and knock : if any man hear My voice, and open the door, I will come in to him.' Of course, that is only the beginning; there is more to follow. After you had accepted your fiancé, you sent announcements to tell your friends that you were engaged. When you accept the Lord Jesus you also tell others that you belong to Him.

"A very important day in your life was your wedding-day. Then you were truly united for better or worse, in joy or in sorrow. When you take Jesus as your Saviour you will step into a world of wealth, the wealth of this Book, the Bible. Then you can claim all of His promises. As you read this Book you will realise that you can be a free and happy child of God when you completely surrender your life to

Him. You cast everything on Him; your sins, your cares, your all. Most wonderful of all is the fact that you must cast your sins upon Him. God is the only one in the whole wide world who can deal with the problem of our sins."

We sat quietly for a few moments, and then together we prayed. She, too, prayed and gave her answer to Jesus— "Yes." Nothing more? No, not for the moment, but when someone for the first time comes to Jesus with an honest "Yes", the angels in heaven rejoice over the soul that has been redeemed.

When I met her the next day she was truly happy and at peace. "I am well aware," she said, "that they can do anything they please with us, even cruelly murder us, but I know also that no one can take out of my heart the peace and happiness that I have found now that I know Jesus lives in my heart."

That same day I met her friend, Mrs. De Goede. "Why not take the same step your friend has taken?" I asked. "See how she has been changed. You, too, can have the same peace."

Her face hardened. "That's not for me. You know nothing of my past. I'm too wicked to be a Christian, one of those pious ones. Oh, no! Being a Christian is all very well for noble souls, but not for me. I'm far too wicked," she repeated.

"Just one moment," I said. "When you read your Bible you will notice there was only one kind of people the Lord could not help—the Pharisees. In their own eyes they were so perfect they needed no Saviour. But sinners were never rejected by the Lord Jesus. To them he said, 'Him that cometh to Me I will in no wise cast out' (John 6 : 37).

"Do you know what the Bible tells us about sins we confess? God drowns them in the depths of the sea. As far as the east is from the west, He casts our sins from us. He throws them away behind Him. He makes them disappear like a cloud. You saw that cloud a moment ago? Now it has disappeared. Where is it? Completely gone! Thus Jesus causes our sins to disappear. John says, 'If we confess our sins, He is faithful and just to forgive us our sins, and to cleanse us from all unrighteousness' (1 John 1 : 9)."

Together we read the parable of the prodigal son, and she,

too, makes the decision for Christ; that decision so necessary for time and eternity, since it means that our names are written in the Book of Life.

It was a few months later that I was standing at the gate of Ravensbruck waiting to be released. When the gate opened I would be free. A friend came to bid me farewell. She took my hand and asked, "Have you heard that Mrs. De Boer and Mrs. De Goede both died today?" Deeply shocked, I gazed once more towards the cruel, bleak camp, and said, "Lord, I thank You that it was Your will to have me here, if only for the sake of those two. But I know You have used Betsie and me to lead many more to Yourself, and that is worth all our suffering, even Betsie's death."

Betsie, my sister, had died a week earlier, but to have been used to save souls for eternity is worth living and dying for.

And now I am in America, in Oak Harbour. Oak Harbour is situated in a remote corner of America, in the extreme north-east. We drive for hours in a car through beautiful country, and now I stand before a small group of people in a tiny church. I relate my experiences as a prisoner and also tell of the conversion of Mrs. De Boer and Mrs. De Goede. The latter's sister is present. She knew that her sister had died somewhere in prison, but it was my lot to cross the ocean and drive across America to an out-of-the-way place to tell her that her sister had been saved for eternity. So is God's way.

Later we sit together on her porch, and she is deeply stirred as she hears the story of her sister's suffering, but also the story of her glorious salvation; saved through Christ Jesus, and translated into glory.

CHAPTER IX

SOPHIE

*"Each redeemed heart is a vast reservoir of potentiality
for God, laid up in store for the drinking of eternal
joys to come."*—Mitchell.

IN a sanatorium in Norton a girl is dying. She has only a
small part of one lung left; an oxygen apparatus helps
her to breathe. It is a joy to be with her. In her room is the
free atmosphere that the approach of death can give where
people are ready to die. She is standing on the edge of
eternity, and it is as if we have a bird's-eye view of earthly
things; we see the reality, and earthly illusions go to the
background.

"Do you know, Corrie, it will be so joyful to work in
heaven. What do you think it will be like?"

"I don't know much, but I believe there will be tremendous activity, without the impediments of this world. We
have to reign with Jesus over the world, and we shall be so
pure, so filled with God's Spirit, that we shall have every
ability to do the work according to His pattern. Here, we
have already got the victory through Jesus Christ, but it is
still a battle against sins. There will be an absolute absence
of sin in Heaven."

"Do you believe that we go immediately to heaven after
we die?"

"The Lord Jesus said to the murderer on the cross, 'Today
shalt thou be with me in Paradise.' His body was still on the
cross the same moment that he was with Jesus in Paradise.
I believe that everyone who dies in Jesus immediately rises
in Paradise. Paul was longing for that when he wrote, 'We
are . . . willing rather to be absent from the body, and to be
present with the Lord' (2 Cor. 5 : 8). He also wrote about the
coming of our Lord for His own, when our bodies will be
resurrected. I think then the souls from Paradise will be
connected with celestial bodies again, and together we will
meet the Lord Jesus in the air."

"Corrie, I know that I have eternal life. 'These things have I written unto you that believe on the name of the Son of God; that ye may know that ye have eternal life' (1 John 5:13), but sometimes I am afraid when I think of the moment of dying. Even the death-beds of children of God can be dark."

"Then pray now that the Lord Jesus will protect you in that moment from the dark powers. That is a prayer which will always be answered. Turn your eyes to the future. Samuel Rutherford wrote in the sixteenth century, 'Our little inch of time of suffering is not worthy of our first night's welcome home to Heaven.' Paul says, 'The sufferings of this present time are not worthy to be compared with the glory which shall be revealed in us' (Rom. 8:18)."

"Corrie, read the beginning of John 14 again."

"Jesus said, 'Let not your heart be troubled: ye believe in God, believe also in Me. In My Father's house are many mansions: if it were not so, I would have told you. I go to prepare a place for you.' Our citizenship is in heaven; we are heavenly citizens. Our home is there. Death is a tunnel. Moody once said, 'In the valley of the shadow of death there must be a light, otherwise there could not be shadow.' Jesus is our light. 'He is able to keep you from falling,' says Jude in verse 24, 'and to present you before His glory without fault and with unspeakable joy' (Phillips). When He holds us, He keeps us; when He keeps us, He guides us; when He guides us, He will one day bring us safely home. When His hand holds us we will not fear, even 'though the earth be removed, and though the mountains be carried into the midst of the sea' (Psa. 46:2)."

"Good-bye, Corrie, until we meet again, when we will be translated to meet the Lord in the sky."

CHAPTER X

TELL ME OF JESUS

"Oh, use me, Lord, use even me. Just as Thou wilt, and when, and where."

O N the platform the choir, in brownish-red gowns, stands behind me; a lady in a white gown is conducting. I can study her while she conducts the choir. Her appearance is unusual. She wears a lot of jewellery, and gracefully moves her beautiful arms, which are decorated with diamond bracelets. She wears brilliant rings on her fingers; her nails are red. Her shoes are transparent. But the most unusual thing about her is her smile. She smiles in a coquettish manner when the tenors make a mistake, encouragingly when a passage is difficult, and coquettishly again when she has nothing else to do.

It is strange to see such a worldly woman taking part in the sacred service. Looking at her, she appears to me to be representative of the movie world, where coquettish women play a big part. Suddenly she sings together with the choir. She has a beautiful voice. Although she stands with her back to the congregation, her solo can be heard above the voices of the choir. For a time I am so absorbed in her appearance that I do not hear what they are singing. Now I listen to the words. She sings, 'Tell me of Jesus.'

My mind wanders. I am no longer in the church. Those words go round and round in my mind. Hollywood demands, "Tell me of Jesus." The sentenced-to-death, desperate, painted society asks, "Tell me of Jesus."

When some moments later I stand before the congregation to bring them my message, in my heart there is a longing—a prayer. "Let me, this woman, and the movie world in Hollywood, tell of Jesus; of Him who came because the Father loved this poor, bad, desperate world."

Because of my background of imprisonment and world travelling, I sometimes arrive at places where doors do not open easily.

I stand before a hearth. In front of me sit fifty movie stars. The Hollywood Christian Group are having their Gospel meeting. About twenty of their members are present; the rest are friends and acquaintances who do not yet know the Lord. We are in the house of a rich movie star. One of those present has a strong lamp which she focuses on me and studies the effect.

I speak about the great love of God in Jesus Christ who can lift us out of the old vicious circle of sin and death. The Holy Spirit convinces us of sin, righteousness, and judgment. The greatest sin is not believing in Jesus.

After the meeting, little groups of people form. I see that the Christians are active and busy with open Bibles showing their colleagues the way of salvation.

I go with a young woman for a little walk on the terrace. She has many questions to ask. Passing a window, I see two young men on their knees. One is a member of the Christian Group, the other a movie star who is making the decision that makes angels rejoice.

What a joy that God answers prayer!

CHAPTER XI

EGOTISM

"My thoughts are not your thoughts, neither are your ways My ways, saith the Lord."—(Isaiah 55 : 8.)

At Havana, in Cuba, I am to speak at a youth rally in the Salvation Army hall. It is very hot, and the hall is small. The meeting begins at seven o'clock, but more and more groups continue to arrive from other parts of the town. Two men have huge drums, and I am sitting on the platform between them. An old Negro with white hair tries to show his love for the Lord by vigorously beating one of the drums. The sound is almost unbearable. The Captain has a very sharp voice, and the young Cubans sing loudly, with much clapping of hands. By nine o'clock I am feeling weary and my head is aching, but while I am speaking it is quiet in the hall, and I am thankful for this chance to give my message, which is followed by a missionary showing slides.

He is a little bit proud of his medical work, for which he has not studied specifically, but he, like all missionaries, must know enough to be able to act in cases of emergency. He has photographs of tables full of drugs. "These were given to me by Dr. Smith," he tells us. The young people in the hall are not at all interested in seeing these boxes, bottles, and phials, and the noise they are making grows to such a volume that the missionary has to shout to make himself heard at all. It is half-past ten by the time he has finished.

Now the Captain gives an invitation to people to come to the front and be saved. A terribly selfish thought comes into my head, "I hope that nobody comes to the front. I long to go to bed."

Twenty young people come out. I see tears in the eyes of a young Cuban. The officer next to him speaks with great persuasion; his voice is full of love.

I am shocked by my selfishness. I had hoped that nobody would be saved because my own sleep was more important than the salvation of sinners. What a terrible egotist I am! But what a joy that I know what to do with my sin. I confess it to my heavenly Father in Jesus' name, and He forgives and cleanses me. Then with joy I can pray for the twenty young people who have made the important decision. It is half-past eleven when the meeting comes to a close.

The next morning I am standing in a beautifully-designed church which the most prominent people of Havana attend. In the parish magazine, given to everyone who enters, I read an introductory article on Corrie ten Boom. It says: "Most popular world evangelist . . . tireless and completely selfless in her absolute dedication to the cause of the Gospel . . . !" Before I give my message, I cannot help reading the introduction aloud, and continue, "Sometimes I get a headache from the heat of the halo that people put around my head. Would you like to know what Corrie ten Boom is really like?" And then I tell them what happened the evening before; of how my own sleep was more important in my eyes than the salvation of young people. "That," I say, "is Corrie ten Boom. What egotism! What selfishness! But the joy is that Corrie ten Boom knows what to do with her sins. When we confess our sins to the heavenly Father, we experience that our Advocate lives—Jesus Christ. He takes our sins on Himself."

Suddenly there is contact with the congregation. We are no longer a beautiful church with prominent members and a popular world evangelist, but we are all sinners who know that Jesus died to lift us out of the vicious circle of sin and death.

CHAPTER XII

SAN BARTOLO DE LA BARRANCA

Life is too short to be little.

"WHAT do you use that knife for?"
    "To defend myself against robbers and wild animals; but today I have to cut the cacti which can be dangerous to the clothing and the skin of Miss Corrie ten Boom."

I follow the Mexican with his big hat and his long knife. I have never seen such a long knife before. It is very sharp, and pieces of cacti fall around him until we reach the edge of the canyon. Far down below, people are working to make a way to a town in the valley. This was once the centre of crime, of murder and theft. It was so difficult to reach that only a few people knew of its existence. Then about eight years ago, God gave some Christians the idea to go and live there, where "Satan's seat" was (Rev. 2 : 13). They could reach the town only by a very tiring journey on horseback through woods and dangerous cliffs.

The first thing they did was to rent the public-house for a meeting. When customers came, they told them, "Wait until we have finished with you!" The persecution they had to suffer was terrible, but they stood their ground. Within a short time God performed miracles, and now it is a Christian town. The mayor is the minister; the judge is his assistant, and all the policemen are deacons.

Although it is rather far away, I can see a huge flat church. It is a strange building, but with room for many. The people saw the dangers of isolation, and tried to make contact with other Christians, whom they invited to come and see them. The bravest of these found a chance to visit the town, but the trip on horseback was dangerous and unbelievably difficult. So the Christians promised their visitors that if they would try to come back the following year they would make a way through the jungle.

This plan was made known, and the Government of the State asked if it was true that Christians were making a

highway through the jungle, though "highway" is too good
a name for the rough road they hacked through the wilder-
ness. The Christians were glad to give information to the
Government, and said that they were willing to work without payment, but that they had no money to cover the costs.
The Government official was so impressed that he promised
material and intructors to help with the work.

The main work is under the supervision of the instructors;
dynamite and tools have been given by the State, and the
Christians from 130 different congregations co-operate in
doing the work. Each congregation contributes one week's
labour. Women come together with the men to cook for
them and take care of them. A text is painted on a rock in
huge letters, "WE WORK FOR GOD AND NOT FOR MEN".

In this Roman Catholic country Protestants are sometimes in a difficult position. Already the work of these
faithful Christians has caused the Government to see with
amazement how useful they can be to society. A congress of
mayors was invited to see the work, and on that day the
first bridge was opened; on it is carved, "WHAT YOU DO, DO
WITH YOUR WHOLE HEART".

An old man with a long beard takes me to the workers.
He climbs with difficulty down the steep mountain. When
the men in the valley see us they shout, "Hallelujah!" and
we answer with the same salute. The sound echoes between
the mountains, "Hallelujah! Hallelujah! Hallelujah!"

In the camp where the women live a meal has been made
for us. One woman rolls a stone over the corn while another
bakes the flat tortillas. The whole camp is rather dirty, but
the atmosphere is happy, and what faithfulness!

"Do all the members of the church come to take their part
in the work?" I ask.

"Yes! But if one did fail, another immediately would take
his place. They say, 'We work because we love God and our
neighbours, and we will serve society.'"

Within two years there will be a highway connecting
San Bartolo de la Barranca with the big world. Poverty
will decrease when there is the possibility of trade, but
people expect far more than that: that this town will be a
pleasing example to all who come into contact with it.

When I leave, I say a few words of farewell—1 John 5 : 4,

5 : "This is the victory that overcometh the world, even our faith. Who is he that overcometh the world, but he that believeth that Jesus is the Son of God?" Here is a little foretaste of the millennium, when the children of God will reign on this earth with Jesus Christ, and the whole world shall be "full of the knowledge of the Lord, as the waters cover the sea".

CHAPTER XIII

WIENER ROAST

"He that winneth souls is wise."—Prov. 11 : 30.

IN America when people go for a picnic they travel by car. How unlike the Europeans, who walk and carry their knapsacks on their backs. Sometimes I fear that Americans are unable to walk! Their cars take them everywhere.

I go to a "wiener roast" with the youth groups of a church. We cook the wieners (sausages) over the fire on spiked sticks cut from the trees. It is a jolly group of people. After the picnic we sit around the fire and the conversation is about soul-winning. A girl student says, "I am no evangelist, and have no guidance to go to a Bible school, but I speak with a lot of young people whom I like to help. Do you know of a good book about soul-winning?"

"Yes, several. One is *The Consuming Fire*, by Oswald J. Smith. He writes a chapter called 'Evangelism in the Enquiry Room', which is a short but powerful guide for soul-winning in personal conversation.

"First, he says, never argue. Many people will try to argue to avoid the important thing. They ask the most impossible questions. Don't try to answer them. Promise to do that later, but first show them that they need salvation.

"Also, trust the Holy Spirit. Only He can convince of sin, and change people—you can't.

"Pray a great deal. Pray before, during, and after your conversation. It is possible that you need exercise, but you can have the horizontal and the vertical connection at the same time.

"Make your diagnosis and seek the remedy. Let the Bible speak.

"Sometimes you can find four groups—the unsaved, the backsliders, the uncertain, and the defeated.

"First, the unsaved, who do not know the Lord Jesus Christ can be their personal Saviour; who do not call them-

selves Christians. They must be invited to repent. Read
with them John 1:12, 'But as many as received Him, to
them gave He power to become the sons of God, even to
them that believe on His name.'

"Then the backsliders. They have slid away from the
Lord. They have lost their first love and are cold in their
work for the Gospel, neglect their Bible reading and prayer,
and never witness. Some live totally in the world. They
must be brought back again to fellowship with God. The
reason for their backsliding is always sin. Read with them
1 John 1:7–9. Show them that they must confess the sins
that have made them backslide. In case they do not feel
any joy after their confession of sins, tell them to thank God
for forgiveness. Often the joy comes only after they have
given thanks with their hands on the promises of the Bible.

"The third group is the uncertain—those who do not
know if they are saved or lost. They have no assurance of
salvation, feeling one day that they are children of God, and
the next that they are lost. They are in a state of permanent
uncertainty. They must be invited to come back because
they have no value for God until they know that they have
passed from darkness into light. Tell them that they must
not trust their feelings, but God's Word.

> Feelings come, and feelings go,
> And feelings are deceiving.
> My warrant is the Word of God
> None else is worth believing.

Let them read 1 John 5:13, 'These things have I written
unto you that believe on the name of the Son of God : that
ye may know that ye have eternal life, and that ye may
believe on the name of the Son of God.' Not feelings, or
wonderful emotional experiences, or unusual revelations,
but 'It is written.'

"What is written cannot be changed. Feelings and
emotions can change. Teach them to act on the Word. Christians are not always on the mountain-top. If there were no
valleys, there could be no mountains. If our feelings were
the foundation, then we could be a child of God only if we
were on the mountain. John says, 'These things have I
written.' What has he written? 'That ye know that ye have
eternal life.' Not that you may have everlasting life some

day, but that you have it here and now. It is very important to show the uncertain these things in the Word of God. God can't use uncertain people. Those who have no assurance of salvation can't help others. They must know that they have passed from darkness into light, and that knowledge comes by faith in what the Bible says.

"Then we have the defeated. Show them 1 Cor. 15 : 57, 'Thanks be to God, which giveth us the victory through our Lord Jesus Christ.' Not by trying hard, by our endeavours or our energy, but by Him, our Lord. Victory is a gift just like salvation—we can't earn it. God gives it to us by His Son. Even Paul cried, 'O wretched man that I am! who shall deliver me from the body of this death?' (Rom. 7 : 24), but immediately adds, 'I thank God through Jesus Christ our Lord.'

"We have accepted Jesus as our Saviour; now we must accept Him as our Victor. When we do this He lives His victorious life in us—He the vine, we the branches. The branch without the vine has no value, but the vine has ever-lasting value. When connected with the vine, the branch gets the same nature, and life, and zeal to bear fruit like the vine itself. 'Without Me ye can do nothing,' Jesus says. But I can do everything through Christ, who gives me strength. Hallelujah !!"

During our talk, the fire has died down. We see clearly the beautiful starry sky. Before we leave, we sing together :

Is your life a channel of blessing?
Is the love of God flowing through you?
Are you telling the lost of the Saviour?
Are you ready His service to do?

Make me a channel of blessing today,
Make me a channel of blessing, I pray;
My life possessing, my service blessing,
Make me a channel of blessing today.

CHAPTER XIV

INGREDIENTS FOR PRAYER

All promises of God are in Jesus, yea and amen.

IN the cell of a prison a woman lies on her cot with a bored expression on her face. She has a cheap novel in her hand, but it does not interest her much. Her needlework lies neglected on her chair. It is warm, and it is Sunday. Does she miss her daily work, which, although monotonous, helps her to get through the day? She is Dutch, but has not attended my meeting.

I am visiting the cells after the sermon—an unusual privilege. Although I am allowed to speak at meetings in prisons, the follow-up work is usually left to the regular prison evangelists. I sit near the Dutchwoman, and for a short time can share her life in the small cell—colourless, monotonous, without any view. I know so well what it is like from my own experience. I feel such great love and compassion for this woman, and pray that the Lord will give me entrance to her heart.

The ice is broken sooner than I expect, and we have a heart-to-heart talk. To begin with, the conversation is about baking cakes—a typical reaction engendered by the hunger which results from a monotonous diet. Carefully I try to turn our talk to deeper things. I discover that she has quite a good knowledge of the Bible, and it is easy to speak to her about the eternal truths. She knows that Jesus died for her on the cross, but she is a backslider.

"Do you sometimes make use of the time that you are alone to pray?" I ask.

"I don't know how to pray. Tell me something of your own prayer life."

"For cakes you need ingredients, and you need them for prayer, too. For instance, the ingredients of a prayer could be :

"1. The promises of God.
"2. Our problems and needs.
"3. Faith to bring these two together.

"If you don't understand me, I'll give you an example.

"Yesterday I was in darkness—really depressed. I didn't know what to do. When this happens I quietly spend a few minutes trying to find the reason. I can imagine a rich lady once a week gathering her bills together, and writing out her cheques. My Bible is my cheque-book; my cares and problems are the bills. The Devil tells me that the Bible is frozen capital, but he is a liar. All promises of God are in Jesus, yea and amen. I asked God to show me the reason for the darkness. God will give His children a clear answer when they are willing to listen in obedience. It is a question of making use of the Quiet Time. Then I wrote down the thoughts that came into my head. Finding the reason for the darkness is in itself a work of liberation. After making my list I took my Bible to 'pay my bills'.

"The first thing I had written was that I was afraid for my health. Next week I must go to Japan, and I wondered if my body would stand the different climate—I am no longer young. I read Romans 8 : 11 (Phillips), 'Nevertheless, once the Spirit that raised Jesus from the dead lives within you that same Spirit will bring to your whole being new strength and vitality.' I said, 'Thank You, Lord. That is for me.' That 'Thank You' meant that I had endorsed a cheque.

"The next thing on my list was that I was feeling down-hearted. The church where I am speaking this week had organised a prayer meeting. I went to that meeting, but nobody else arrived. I had to pray alone. Then I read Romans 8 : 27b (Phillips), 'The Spirit prays for those who love God', and verse 34, 'Christ prays for us'. I understood then that there *had* been a prayer meeting, for if you are praying, the Lord is praying, and the Holy Spirit is praying, and that makes a prayer cell. I said, 'Thank You, Lord', and another bill was paid.

"Thirdly, there followed my feeling of guilt. I had been tempted to gossip. No, it was not slandering. Everything said was true, but it was negative. Paul writes in Romans 14 (Phillips), 'Why criticise your brother's actions? After all, who are you to criticise the servant of somebody else, especially when that Somebody Else is God? It is to his own Master that he gives, or fails to give, satisfactory service. And don't doubt that satisfaction, for God is well able to transform men into servants who are satisfactory.'

"There were other sins I had committed for the umpteenth time; worry, selfishness, etc. I read Romans 8 : 1 (Phillips), 'No condemnation now hangs over the head of those who are "in" Christ Jesus. For the new spiritual principle of life "in" Christ lifts me out of the old vicious circle of sin and death.' I said, 'Thank You, Lord. The devil is very strong, but You are victor.'

"The last thing I had written down was that deep in my heart I was afraid to go to Japan. I do not know the language, nor what awaits me there. I wondered if people would help me, and if I should be able to find my way about. What a shame to have such doubts. The Lord has carried me through a most terrible time in prison. Won't He take care of me in Japan? I read the words of victory at the end of Romans 8, 'Who shall separate us from the love of Christ? In all these things we are more than conquerors.' My last bill was paid, the cheques written. The darkness was all gone. I saw again that God's promises are greater realities than our problems. How exceedingly rich we are when we do not limit the promises of the Bible by our unbelief."

"When you talk like this, I really start to long to live the Christian life again. I am going to do my best."

I look smilingly at her. "Do you see this stick? Do you think it is possible for it to stand upright on its own? Of course not, for it is not the nature of the stick to stand by itself. It can do so only when my hand keeps it steady. It is not the nature of human beings to be able to stand on their own. They can do it only when they surrender to the hand that will keep them from falling. Look, here in Jude, verse 24 (Phillips), it is written : 'Now to Him who is able to keep you from falling and to present you before His glory without fault and with unspeakable joy.' "

For a moment we are quiet together, and I know that the

Holy Spirit works in her heart. Then she surrenders to the Hand that was wounded to save her.

I write in her Bible :

> It is not try, but trust.
> It is not do, but done.
> Our God has planned for us
> Great victory through His Son.

CHAPTER XV

OBEDIENCE

Our eyes must be turned towards God as the eyes of the musician are turned towards the conductor.

IT is a wonderful life that is guided by a God who never makes mistakes. The only condition laid upon us is obedience.

"When are you going to bring this message to the Japanese?" a friend asks me after he hears one of my lectures. Until then I have worked only in America and Europe, Japan being far from my thoughts.

In my Quiet Time the instruction comes distinctly, "Go to Japan." I almost answer, "Yes, but . . ." Obedience says, "Yes, Lord", and I have learned to obey. I want to say, "Yes, but I know nobody there; I can't speak the language and it is so expensive." Again and again I begin counting and forget that my heavenly Treasurer reckons differently from me. The money comes, enough for a flight to Tokyo, where I arrive safely.

It is raining, and from the air Tokyo looks dark and dreary. I am not at all sure of myself. In the customs office a man asks me where he is to take my suit-case. I tell him I do not know.

"Is someone going to meet you?"

"No; nobody."

He feels sorry for me and offers to find me a hotel.

"Yes, if you please—and if possible one where English, German, or Dutch is spoken."

In his own car he takes me to a hotel. It is small, dirty, and dark, but the manager understands some English. But now there is a conflict in my soul. Was that really God's guidance? What if it was a mistake? I hardly dare to go out of doors for fear I might lose my way back to the hotel. Who would understand me? It becomes a real temptation from Satan. How terribly God's children are tempted in these times. It is as though Satan knows his time is running out. Then I read 1 Peter 1 in Phillips' *Letters to Young Churches* about the glorious inheritance reserved in heaven for me, and in the meantime we are guarded by God's power until we enter fully into that heritage—the only life insurance we can collect after our death.

"This means tremendous joy to you, I know, even though at present you are temporarily harassed by all kinds of trials and temptations. This is *no accident*—it happens to prove your faith, which is infinitely more valuable than gold, and gold as you know, even though it is ultimately perishable, must be purified by fire. This proving of your faith is *planned* to bring you praise and honour and glory in the day when Jesus Christ reveals Himself."

No accident—planned! Not by accident, God's plan? But why? To bring praise and glory on the great day of Christ's return. How glorious to catch a glimpse of that great plan and to see your own troubles as a tiny part of that plan. God makes no mistakes!

How it happens I cannot explain, but trust takes the place of doubt, and I can say, "Lord, I know I am safe in Your everlasting arms. You are guiding me and will surely make the next step plain."

Then comes to mind: "David Morken." Is that God's answer? Years ago I met David at a Youth for Christ meeting, and he told me then that he might be sent to Japan. Fortunately the telephone directory is printed in English, and there is his name, "David Morken, Director of Youth for Christ, Tokyo".

How wonderful, for now the next step is clear. I pick up the telephone and hear a voice saying, "Mashie, mashie, mushie, mushie." In confusion I replace the receiver. I cannot even telephone in this strange land of strange people speaking a strange language. Finally, the manager gets the number for me, and I speak to David Morken.

"Hello. This is Corrie ten Boom speaking."

"What! Where are you?"

"Here in Tokyo."

"With whom?"

"Alone."

"But Corrie, how could you? You can't speak Japanese.

If this isn't just like you, to come alone to a country where you can't understand the language!"

"It isn't my doing. I'm not enjoying this at all. It is God's doing, sending me here."

"OK. Always obey what God tells you to do. I'll help you. Go to the Central Railway Station, and I'll meet you with my car."

He did not offer to come to the hotel because it is hard to locate places in Tokyo. The first house built in a street is No. 1, the second, No. 2, even though it may be half a mile farther down the street. Hence numbers mean nothing.

"How do I find the station?"

"Take a taxi."

"What must I say to the taxi-driver?"

"Ekki." And true enough, I call a taxi and just say, "Ekki," and eventually arrive at the station, where David Morken awaits me. That day I am his guest, after which he secures a room for me in an Inter-Varsity Christian Fellowship house.

The first week I speak three times, the second week eighteen times, and the third week twenty-six times. A season of unusual blessing awaits me. How happy I am that I said, "Yes, Lord," instead of "Yes, but . . ."

One of the greatest blessings in Japan is that God uses me to help His special messengers, the missionaries. I am able to give them inspiration, and show them from my own experiences that Jesus' victory is a greater reality than our problems.

Many missionaries have to spend their first years in Japan learning the language. This period can be very trying, for they cannot play their real part. They go to a heathen land with hearts burning to save souls for eternity, and then they must sit on school benches and learn the difficult language. Let us be very faithful in our intercession for them, for it is a time when many are assailed by doubts as to whether, after all, it really was God's will for them to undertake the work.

AMNESTY

To a group of political prisoners I speak about the forgiveness of sins. The next day a letter written in perfect

Dutch comes with the request, "Will you write to your Queen for me? She is the only one who can grant me amnesty." The writer is one of 260 Japanese prisoners sentenced by the Dutch Government for war crimes in Indonesia, once the Dutch East Indies. They are now in a Japanese prison.

I hardly know what to do. Lacking an answer, I follow Hezekiah's example, when during the siege of Jerusalem he received that threatening letter from Rabshakeh, and "spread it before the Lord".

"What must I do, Lord?" I ask.

The answer comes clearly. "Ask amnesty not only for this man, but for all 260."

I go to the Consul to seek his help in composing my letter, for it is not every day I write to a queen. "These men are guilty," I write, "but in you they see the Christian monarch of a Christian country. Perhaps they can better understand the mercy of our Lord Jesus if you can see your way clear to grant them their freedom, and so it will be to God's glory and honour."

The Queen sends me the answer that she will do her utmost to see that my request is granted, but at least two years expire before the men are freed.

However, that week I am called before the committee responsible for all prisoners in Japan. A permit is given me to speak in all prisons; in fact, an itinerary is mapped out for me. I can count on their full co-operation in appreciation for what I did for their political prisoners. What a blessing! When a missionary or pastor speaks, each inmate is asked whether he is interested in the Christian religion. Often only a handful shows up at meetings. But since my work is considered more or less official, attendance is compulsory for all prisoners, and at times also for the attendants. What an opportunity!

The prisons are often far apart. Life is now very different from what I experienced in Tokyo. In large cities the customs and manners of Europeans are well known, and the Japanese are the most polite people in the world. So, when a guest in a Japanese home, I am often offered a chair; though it is their custom to sit on the floor, and often I find a spoon beside my plate that I may eat in comfortable

European fashion instead of handling chopsticks. But now the carefully laid plan takes me far away from the large cities. A police wagon meets me at the station and carries me to the prison. Frequently I ride in jeeps over rough roads. The bouncing is good exercise, I tell myself, but somehow I do not appreciate it.

Usually a dinner has been prepared in my honour. The warden and officials sit with me on the floor, and we eat with chopsticks. The Japanese are well read, and the conversation is stimulating. They speak of "Het Spinhuis", the reformatory in Amsterdam, where back in the sixteenth century prisoners were not only held but also educated at the same time. They appreciate the Dutch, who even in those early days saw the possibilities, now universally accepted, in educating prisoners. I had hardly expected conversation of this kind in these remote corners of Japan's northernmost island.

"Today you will address one hundred and forty gangsters," the warder warns me. There they sit closely-packed on the floor, long rows of Japanese sitting on their heels. My first reaction is, "What darkness!" Cruel faces stare at me.

The lost ones! The world has only one answer, to keep them behind barbed wire. Then great joy rises in my heart. I have a message for them; the answer to their problems. An ocean of sin and darkness was covered with a greater ocean of love and light when Jesus died upon the cross. It was for them He died and bore the sins of the whole world.

I tell them of this ocean of love. "Your souls are precious in the sight of God. Accept Jesus as your Lord and Saviour and He will give you power to become children of God. The tender father-heart of God yearns for your love."

I can almost see the faces change. I see God's love at work, and His love overflows in my heart as never before. What great riches! The prisoners applaud. It is the only expression allowed them, and their applause is long and loud.

Since there is no hotel, the interpreter and I are guests at the governer's home. At dinner that evening he says, "While you were speaking, the thought came to me that I, too, would like to be saved."

"That is possible. Jesus died for the sins of the whole

world, yours included. Believe on the Lord Jesus Christ and you shall be saved."

"I am thinking of choosing a saviour for myself, but haven't made up my mind whether it shall be Christ or Buddha. It really does not matter which, does it, as long as we are sincere?"

"You think it does not matter?" I pray for wisdom and remember an illustration.

"Two men were building a house. Suddenly the scaffolding broke. One man grabbed a rope that was firmly fastened, and saved his life. The other grabbed a rope also, but it was loose, and he fell with the rope to the ground and was killed. If you choose Jesus as Saviour you will be saved for time and eternity. But if you choose Buddha I fear you will be eternally lost. Do you believe that Buddha is alive?"

His answer is typical. "You will have to ask the Commissioner of Education. He knows all about Buddha—I know nothing about him."

"Do you believe that Jesus lives?"

"Yes; I'm sure of it. I saw it in the prisoners' eyes when you spoke about Him."

"Why, then, is it so difficult to choose? You know Jesus lives and don't know whether Buddha is alive or not."

"No, that choice isn't so difficult," he says, and after we pray he makes the decision that causes the angels in heaven to rejoice.

Later, he asks, "Is there anything else I can do for you?"

"Yes. Perhaps there are prisoners who would like to meet me. I am so eager to help them further. After all, one talk is so little." And indeed there are fourteen who wish to speak to me, and a whole hour is granted me, even though it is against the rules that prisoners leave their cells after five o'clock. I feel I must make the most of every minute.

"Friends, it would take me months to teach you all I feel you should know, but we have just one hour. Tell me, which of you care to make the decision for the Lord of whom John says : 'As many as received Him, to them gave He power to become the sons of God'?"

"We all have; that's why we are here," one replies.

"Very well, there is work to be done. You must be ambassadors for Christ. There are many souls to be rescued for eternity in this prison. I shall send you a Bible and a course of Bible study. To begin with, here are eight selections which you can use to bring others to Christ :

John 1 : 12	Rom. 3 : 23
John 3 : 16	1 Tim. 1 : 15
John 6 : 37b	1 John 1 : 7, 9
John 14 : 6	Rev. 3 : 20

"When you have finished the first Bible study course I shall send you another in soul-winning. In the meantime you must be the intercessors for the rest of the prisoners. For instance, you assemble together at meal-times. Perhaps you could arrange to sit together as Christians and form prayer-cells. Pray together for five minutes, or even one minute if that is all you can manage. Jesus has said, 'Where two or three are gathered together in My name, there am I in the midst of them.'

"I know how you feel when you are alone in your prison cells after five o'clock. I myself spent four months in solitary confinement. That is the time to pray for others. Pray for your fellow-prisoners, especially those to whom you have brought the Gospel. Pray for the attendants and for your dear ones at home, if you still have them. There is much to be done for the Master, but remember He can use only those who are pure in heart. That, too, is possible for you. Just confess your sins. Anyone who confesses his sins will find God faithful to forgive them, and the blood of Jesus cleanses from *all* sin. When you confess, He will give you the new heart in which He wishes to dwell. But you must never, never compromise."

We have a moment of silence and then we give thanks together.

"Now," I ask, "who has given himself unconditionally to the Lord?" Fourteen hands are raised in firm and full surrender.

Fourteen gangsters, murderers ! Fourteen lifers !

Fourteen despised, lost men? No; fourteen ambassadors for Christ.

Shall they one day hear the words, "Well done, thou good and faithful servant : thou hast been faithful over a few things, I will make thee ruler over many things" ?

Shall I see them one day, with those they have brought to the Lord?

A year later I receive a letter with some money enclosed. It is from one of the prisoners. He writes, "I have been unexpectedly set free. I have found work, and the first money I have earned in my freedom I am sending to you. Please send me a Bible. The balance of the money is for your work.

"When you spoke to us in prison I accepted Jesus as my Saviour. I served Him behind the bars, and now I plan to serve Him as a free man."

I write to a missionary commending this former prisoner to the fellowship of a live congregation and suggesting he be put to work there for his Master. What a privilege to see some of the blessed fruit the Vine has given through the branches.

CHAPTER XVI

THE POWER OF JESUS' NAME

"The true child of God is in the charge of God's own Son and the evil one must keep his distance."
—I John 5 :18 (Phillips).

How difficult it is to become used to speaking through interpreters. It is like trying to reach for people round a corner. The listener's eyes being on the interpreter, the speaker is more or less out of touch with his audience. It has one virtue, however; there is time for prayer while speaking.

Today I have an especially fine interpreter. He loves the Lord with all his heart, and it is pure delight to work together—such a contrast to indifferent interpreters. We are guests in the same home, and since we must speak again in the evening there is time to chat together. Suddenly I ask, "Why is there so much darkness in you?"

"What do you mean?"

"There is no joy of the Lord in your eyes. In the parable of the vine and the branches, the Lord says, 'That My joy might remain in you, and that your joy might be full.' Where is that joy?"

"I don't know."

"I think perhaps I know. May I speak? When you were converted from Shintoism to the Lord, you turned your back on demons, but the demons have not turned their backs on you."

In surprise he answers, "That is true. But please don't tell the missionaries. They may think I've gone back to Shintoism."

"Demons are no ism. They are realities even as angels, and as you and I are. What you lack is a knowledge of the riches which are yours. You need not remain in darkness one moment longer. In the name of the Lord Jesus and by the blood of the Lamb we have the victory. In His name you can drive out the demons and withstand Satan."

Together we read and obey the glorious promise and command in Mark 16:15-18, and then the Lord performs the miracle of the complete liberation of His child.

A few weeks later we meet again. "Not only am I free," he says, "but my wife and children also." All hail the power of Jesus' name! The wonderful name of Jesus is all powerful in heaven and on earth. That name above every name.

Many missionaries have *given* their all, money, family, and homeland, but they do not take all the riches offered them in God's Word. Theologically their training has often been basic, but would not a study of God's Word teaching them to cast out demons and heal the sick make them more fruitful?

How many dark powers there are in the world! Yet we have nothing to fear. The fear of demons is from the demons themselves. We overcome by the blood of the Lamb, and His blood protects us. And what joy it is that we have the authority of the name of Jesus.

Those who are with us are far more than those who are against us. At our side is our mighty High Priest and His legions of angels.

CHAPTER XVII

THAT INTERCESSION BE MADE

I measure my influence by the number who need my prayers and the number who pray for me.

Tokyo is noisy. Loudspeakers screaming shrill music in the streets sound above the hubbub below. Opposite the house where I live is a school of music. It is July and steaming hot. Windows are wide open everywhere, and the mingled sounds of trumpets, harmonicas, and violins fling their clamour into my hot room. It is almost unbearable. Evenings are hours of affliction, for all things seem to work together for evil. Previously I lived with four missionaries, one a woman who, with the help of a Japanese girl, took charge of the cooking. We had delightful meals due more to the fine fellowship around the tiny table in that small room with its mat-covered floor than to the quality of the food. Happily for me I could throw off the burden of past experiences as together we read the Bible, related difficulties, and praised the Lord for blessings shared with His children.

But now I am alone. The others have left for a cooler climate in the hills while I must complete several series of lectures in the university, a Bible seminary, and a students' club. I try cooking in the queer kitchen, but have not much success. I am not very skilled in the science of cooking, and evidently the Japanese idea of hygiene differs from mine, for somehow everything I cook tastes of fish. A cockroach scuttles from the wardrobe after chewing holes in my very best dress. I begin to lose heart.

The nights seem unendurably hot. The unscreened window invite swarms of mosquitoes. Self-pity rises in my heart and whispers, "Why must I work here when the heat is so overpowering? I'm no longer young, and adjustment does not come easily. Why must I be alone? Why? Why? It's just too bad, Corrie!"

Self-pity creates darkness, and can even cause sickness. It

is a very respectable sin, logical and convincing, and places self on the throne.

One evening all the neighbours turn up their radios to drown the cacophony from the school of music. It is too much. No human being can bear this!

Suddenly I look into the mirror and burst out laughing. What a long face! How foolish to feel so sorry for myself. I try singing above the clamour, and sure enough, it works. The heat of the night can be endured, after all, for a prayer rises in my heart, "Lord Jesus, You suffered so much to save me from sin and make me a child of Yours. Why shouldn't I endure a bit of discomfort in carrying Your message to others? It is well, Lord. You had no place to lay Your head. I have a bed, and a room, even though they are both filled with mosquitoes."

A fortnight later a letter from Toronto reaches me. A friend writes, "Today an acquaintance 'phoned and asked me if I knew you. I told her we were friends. She has never met you but has just finished reading your book *Amazing Love*, and since then has been in prayer for you all day long. I asked her to visit me, and together we prayed for you."

Is it not wonderful! We read in Isaiah 59:16, "And God wondered that there was no intercessor." How important is intercession. In Tokyo a child of God loses heart and falls into the sin of self-pity. Of course God can save her, but first He sends a command to Toronto, "Pray for her." And not until two of His children obey does He rescue Corrie ten Boom in Tokyo.

So are God's ways.

CHAPTER XVIII

THE LILY OF THE VALLEY CLUB

IN a street in Japan I meet some boys and girls with baskets full of tracts and Gospels of John. They seek to leave in every home a Gospel and a tract. They work to a well-organised plan, and after they have spent every Saturday afternoon for ten months each house in Nagaoka will have had a Gospel of John.

They are just children, but the Lord uses them. They call themselves "The Lily of the Valley Club". The leader is an eighteen-year-old boy, Daniel. He was once an opium smoker. The moment that he received the Lord Jesus he was free, and now works full-time for the Lord and the church.

In one of the houses is a woman who years ago was a Christian, but she has turned away from the Lord. She finds the Gospel of John and starts to read. The Holy Spirit uses this reading, and later she calls her husband and children and tells them what she has read. She visits the minister, and now the whole family goes to church.

In heaven The Lily of the Valley Club will hear from several sides, "It was you who invited me here!"

There is a Bible woman who visits every week sixteen different villages to bring them the Gospel. She is a sick woman with tuberculosis in both lungs.

"I can't go to bed and be ill as long as there are so many people who don't know the Lord," she says to me.

What heroes there are in God's kingdom!

A little boy, Steven, cannot yet go to school because he is too young; only five years old. He is a clever little man, and therefore his mother, an American missionary, teaches him the Japanese language to keep him busy. Steven tells me, "I learn Japanese because I'll be a missionary."

"What about Russia, Steven? Won't you be a missionary there?"

"Sure I will!" says the little boy.

"But then you must learn Russian also. Are you willing?"

"Mummy, don't you think it is better that I wait until I am six?"

CHAPTER XIX

THE WINNING BLOW

If you will work for God, form a committee.
If you will work with God, form a prayer group.

DURING my trip from Formosa to Australia, I am able to stay for five days in Hong Kong. This beautiful island has riches and poverty side by side. It has the most beautiful window displays in the world, but also many slums full of refugees. It is a piece of free China with huge problems.

My time there is full of activity. I am in contact with many consecrated Christians. The meetings are extremely well organised, every minute of the day being put to good use.

One evening the Holy Spirit is obviously working in a group of young Christians who some time ago accepted Jesus Christ as their Saviour. On this particular evening they come to a full surrender, and accept Him as their Victor. "Thanks be to God, which giveth us the victory through our Lord Jesus Christ" (1 Cor. 15 : 57).

One asks, "What is expected of us now?"

"The Lord will show you. Wait patiently for His guidance. But there is one thing I can advise you to do now, and that is to organise prayer cells. Prayer is not a prefix or a suffix; it is central. Over the whole world I see that God gives His children prayer cells. It is not only the Communists who form cells, but wherever two or three come together in Jesus' name, there is a cell for Him. In eternity we shall see how important prayer meetings have been."

A group of students in Chicago prayed every week for a number of unsaved fellow-students. Eventually everyone on the list was saved. One of them was Dr. Torrey Johnson, the founder of Youth for Christ. Wherever I have travelled over the world I have seen how this work has been blessed. Thousands and tens of thousands have found their Saviour through it. What was the first cause? Torrey Johnson? No; the prayers of those young men in Chicago. Intercession is so tremendously important that in Isaiah 59 : 16 is written, "God wondered that there was no intercessor."

"If you will work for God, form a committee. If you will work with God, form a prayer group."

That evening, we make plans for a weekly prayer meeting, and later I hear that more have commenced. The greatest thing we can do for one another is to pray. Prayer is striking the winning blow at the concealed enemy—our service is gathering up the results.

CHAPTER XX

BOOMERANG

The first step on the way to victory is to recognise the enemy.

AT a conference of Bible school students it is necessary to have somebody to interpret for me, and this is done by a girl who finds it difficult to understand my English. When I use an illustration involving radar in ships she becomes quite mixed up, as she has never heard of radar before. I try to help her, and say :

"It doesn't matter; we will try something else. A captain of a ship stood on the bridge . . ." but she has never heard of the bridge of a ship, and does not say a word. I tell her, "Read Phillips' translation of James 1 : 5. 'If any of you does not know how to meet any particular problem he has only to ask God—who gives generously to all men without making them feel foolish or guilty—and he may be quite sure that the necessary wisdom will be given him.' You lack the wisdom to interpret for Corrie ten Boom. This is the address where you can get it."

But it is too late. She bursts into tears. A Japanese who loses face is lost; you cannot do anything with him. I ask the leader of the conference if there is another interpreter, but he tells me there is not. So here I am, with a message for the young people before me. Some of them have problems, and the answers can be found in the Bible that I have in my hand.

For what reason am I unable to bring God's message to them? Here is the devil at work. The first step on the way to victory is to recognise the enemy. The devil is a conquered enemy, and we have the privilege and the authority to fight him in the name of the Lord Jesus. I turn to the girl and say :

"Dark power that hinders this girl from interpreting God's message—I command you in the name of the Lord Jesus to leave her alone. She is meant to be a temple of the Holy Spirit, not your temple."

As I speak, the girl is set free. She is able to interpret fluently, and we have a meeting that is greatly blessed. So what the devil has meant to be an illustration of his victory becomes a boomerang and shows the power of Jesus Christ and His name.

CHAPTER XXI

LAILANI

Do not be a victim of activity. When Satan cannot make you bad, he makes you busy.

Honolulu is a beautiful island. What riches of sun and colour! Nature gives an overflow of flowers the whole year round. The blue water, the mountains—it really makes a symphony in clear colours. Young people decorate themselves with flower chains sometimes made of beautiful orchids, and these they also wear in their hair. Their clothing is multi-coloured. The life of the tourist is frivolous, but I come into contact more with the Christians, who educate their children carefully and keep them away from the tourist world. There are several Bible-study and prayer groups.

One evening the conversation is about prayer. Lailani says, "I think it is very difficult to pray."

"No wonder. Even the disciples did not find it easy. They asked the Lord to teach them how to pray. It is a strategic point. The devil smiles when we are up to our ears in work, but he trembles when we pray. Sometimes I think that there must be a map of the world both in heaven and in hell. The most important points on the map are not the Kremlin in Moscow, or the Pentagon building in Washington, but the places where two or three or more are gathered in Jesus' name in prayer meetings."

When the Americans entered Germany after the War, a law was made forbidding fraternisation. In one minister's family were two teen-age children. At school they had heard terrible things about the Americans. One day the girls saw an American officer coming towards their house, and cried, "Look, father. He is coming to our house."

"Don't be afraid. Americans are not barbarians."

The officer entered the house, and when he came into their room, said, "We are forbidden to speak and eat together, but nobody has forbidden us to pray together."

He knelt down, and the minister and his family followed.

Into the hearts of the children at that moment came a great love for the Americans. Prayer is like Jacob's ladder. Angels go up and down, but it is God who places the ladder.

"But I find I have no time to pray," says Lailani.

"You remind me of a German minister with far too big a congregation who said he was really too busy to pray. He had plenty of theology but no 'kneeology'. That is just as fruitless as a beautiful lamp without electricity.

"My full schedule and constant travelling from one place to another can sometimes bring me into the same danger. In the morning I must awaken early to travel; in the evening I roll into bed dead tired. On such occasions I have really tried to find time to pray until I have seen that prayerlessness is a sin. I know what to do with sins. I do not try to overcome them, but face them, and 1 John 1 : 7 and 9 gives the answer. A sin confessed to the Lord is a sin forgiven; a sin forgiven is a sin cleansed. In the same moment that I confessed my prayerlessness I found time to pray.

"Trying to catch up on our prayers while sitting in the bus or train or aeroplane after the day's work has begun is a poor substitute. We must begin the day by tuning our instruments with the help of the great Conductor. Prayer is the key for the day; the lock for the night. When Satan cannot keep us from doing work for the Lord he comes behind us and pushes us into doing too much work, and much we do is not right. In that case we must pray with the coloured man who was too busy, and who said :

> Slow me down, Lord, I'm going too fast,
> I can't see my brother when he's going past;
> I miss a lot of good things day by day,
> I can't see a blessing when it comes my way.

"You can do more than praying after you have prayed. You can never do more than praying before you have prayed."

After our conversation we sing with a group :

> Drop Thy still dews of quietness,
>   Till all our strivings cease;
> Take from our souls the strain and stress,
> And let our ordered lives confess
>   The beauty of Thy peace.

Lailani sings with us, and I know that her heart prays.

CHAPTER XXII

A LEPER COLONY

"Little children, abide in Him; that, when He shall appear, we may have confidence, and not be ashamed before Him at His coming."—1 John 2 : 28.

IN Formosa is a Government leper colony where a courageous missionary, Mrs. Dixon, does miracles. Before she went there the lepers had to take care of themselves, and lived huddled together in the greatest misery. She brought new sleeping-mats and put planks around the cots so that the rats could not easily reach them. Together with the lepers, she built paths so that their wounded feet could walk with greater comfort. She convened committees from the lepers who were still able to help those who had no fingers left to cook for themselves. German nurses work there now, and many improvements have been made. There is now healing for those in the initial stages of the disease, for new drugs do miracles for them, but most of the cases are too far advanced. Life is made much happier by the provision of a library and recordings of good music. The cases of suicide are now much fewer since the poor lepers began to realise that there are people who care for them. The crown of her work is a church on the hill, where every day the Christians gather together.

I try to spend all my spare time working in the leper colony. At first I am scared. I fear infection. But when I see how the other people work without any fear, I am ashamed, and I visit the sick who cannot go to church. It is a joy to lead the meetings. There is a hunger for the Gospel. When I speak about the ocean of the love of God in Jesus Christ their faces beam with joy. One man especially catches my eye because of his radiant countenance, although his face itself is repulsive—the disease has destroyed his nose. This man is one of the courageous witnesses for Christ, and has brought more than fifty other people to the Lord.

On one occasion an evangelist was speaking to these lepers

from the text, "Abide in Him; that, when He shall appear, we may have confidence, and not be ashamed before Him at His coming" (1 John 2 : 28).

He asked, "Are any of you afraid that if Jesus should come today you would feel ashamed?"

One man put up his hand—it was the courageous soul-winner.

"Why are you afraid?"

"I have done so little for the Lord."

What a lesson for so many Christians who do little or nothing to bring other people to the Lord. This man is a leper—a mortally ill man, but he does what he can, and he is so humble. When he reaches heaven many people will say to him, "You have invited me here."

When I leave the camp many lepers stand at the gate. They are not allowed to leave the camp. Some are soldiers who have a red cross on their uniforms to show that they have leprosy, and are prisoners in the colony like the others. Every day when I go they wave their hands—some hands are without fingers—and sing, "Don't be afraid of what may come. Our Father cares for you."

CHAPTER XXIII

RESISTANCE

Faith brings us on highways that make our reasoning dizzy.

IT is a joy to work in Formosa because the Chinese are more free and open than the Japanese. The people in Japan can take politeness to such extremes that often you do not know what they really think. They believe that the worst that can ever happen is to lose face, and they have the same fear for their guests. That is why most of the time they agree with everything said—just out of politeness.

The Chinese are different. They can be very impolite.

At a theological school I say something that irritates the students. I tell them that it is all wrong to be studying theology without believing the Gospel. I show them the danger of teaching the Word of God without having faith in it themselves. It may be that on God's judgment day we will find that those who have taught without faith have led many souls astray and have much to answer for.

A whole row of students take their books at that moment and begin ostentatiously writing to show very clearly that they are no longer willing to listen.

This is the last of my lectures in this school, and it is a failure. Have I done wrong? Can God perhaps hit straight with a crooked stick and bless His Word even when it is taught by unbelievers? If only I could have another opportunity to speak. During that week I pray a great deal for the students.

One morning the telephone rings.

"We have been waiting for a speaker, but it seems that he is unable to come. Will you take his place in the theological school?"

Here is the answer. I have just enough time to ask some of my friends to remain in prayer for as long as I shall be speaking.

When I get there I take the bull by the horns and say,

"Gentlemen, you have clearly shown me that you did not agree with my last lecture. Will you please be polite enough not to start reading or writing, but to listen to what God has to tell you? Pray that He will speak, and that the Holy Spirit will work so that all of us can understand not what Corrie ten Boom has to say, but what He has to say."

And now the Lord gives me a message. It is not weaker than the last one. I do not take back what I said, but there is more love and understanding in my words. I see that everyone listens, and there is a great blessing.

"The Bible is not like other books. It is the Word of God, the sword of the Spirit. We must handle it with reverence. When we read and teach it under the guidance of God's Spirit, it is a sharp two-edged sword. Paul shows us this very clearly in the first two chapters of 1 Corinthians. He tells us there is a difference between faith knowledge and sense knowledge. What we see by faith is an invisible reality, much more important than our logical thinking. Faith brings us on to highways that make our reasoning dizzy. Just imagine a captain who is unable to believe in his radar and is unwilling to use it in navigating, but instead depends upon his own eyes and what they can see. His ship would be involved in a severe collision in foggy weather. The foolishness of God is so much more important than the wisdom of the wise.

"Bringing the Gospel is the Holy Spirit speaking through us. Whoever comes to God must believe that He is. Even psychology shows us that it is impossible to teach the Gospel without believing in it. A good business-man has faith in his products. A doctor believes in the drugs he prescribes; and it is still more important that God's Word brings us into holy territory. We cannot play God's music if we are not tuned in by the Holy Spirit to His heavenly harmony. The Lord Jesus says, 'Except a man be born again, he cannot see the Kingdom of God.' "

What a joy that God answers prayers, and that He gave me this extra hour. After the lecture there is a blessed discussion, and I know that God will perform what He began to do that morning.

CHAPTER XXIV

NO UNEQUAL YOKE

It is costly to accept, but it is far more costly to reject.

Two girls come to me for advice, and they tell me their difficulties.

One says, "I am a Christian. My parents are Buddhists. When they go to the temple to worship at the shrine they expect me to go with them. I do not believe in Buddha, and I want to know if it is wrong for me to go with them without believing in what they say there. I go to make my parents happy, and do not believe it can do me any harm."

I pray for wisdom, and then tell her, "The Lord Jesus has bought you with His blood—a high price. He has a legal right to possess you wholly. You can never make a compromise with Him. He Himself says, 'No man can serve two masters.' Do you lose something by accepting that? Yes, it means that for Jesus' sake you lose your life, but you win a far better life. Is it costly to accept? Yes, but it is far more costly to reject."

The other girl tells me of an almost greater conflict. "I am engaged to be married to a Buddhist. He thinks it is all right for me to follow Jesus. He allows me to go to church, and has promised me that when we are married he will give me complete freedom. What do you think of that?"

"The Bible says it is not possible to be unequally yoked with an unbeliever. Do you know what an unequal yoke is? Two animals of unequal strength put together to pull a cart are dragging against each other in an unequal yoke, and that makes suffering for both. It is really an impossibility. The Lord Jesus makes Himself very clear in this. Those who will follow Him must belong to Him, and follow Him in everything. He who loses His life for Jesus' sake has Him as Lord and King in every part of his life, and is, therefore, a yoke-fellow with Jesus. What riches! With Him we are more than conquerors."

After we have prayed together, both the girls surrender

their whole lives into the hands of the Saviour—an absolute surrender.

A month later, I meet a sister of one of these girls in Hong Kong. She tells me, "Since their surrender both of the girls are so intensely happy. Their letters are full of joy. One wrote to say that she has told her fiancé she cannot marry him, and there is now a great peace in her heart."

What is total surrender? A joyful experience.

> And shall I pray Thee change Thy will, O Father,
> Until it is according unto mine?
> But no, Lord, no, that never shall be. Rather
> I pray Thee, blend my human will with Thine.

His yoke is easy. His burden is light.

> He knows, He loves, He cares,
> Nothing this truth can dim,
> He gives the very best to those,
> Who leave the choice to Him.

Eugenia Price writes, "I have found that Jesus Christ never asks us to give up a single thing which He doesn't replace with good measure, pressed down and running over."

A coloured man saw his little boy carrying a load far too heavy for him. He took in one hand the load and in the other hand the little boy.

Total surrender is like that—safe in the hands of Jesus.

CHAPTER XXV

MARTYRDOM

"As thy days, so shall thy strength be."—Deut. 33 : 25.

ANNIE FLINT composed this poem :

> He giveth more grace when the burden grows greater,
> He sendeth more strength when the labours increase,
> To added affliction He addeth His mercy,
> To multiplied trials, His multiplied peace.
>
> When we have exhausted our store of endurance,
> When faith seems to fail ere the day is half gone,
> When we come to the end of our hoarded resources,
> Our Father's full giving is only begun.
>
> His love has no limit, His grace has no measure,
> His power has no boundary known unto men,
> For out of His infinite riches in Jesus,
> He giveth, and giveth, and giveth again.

How much will we Christians have to suffer for our faith?
The Chinese of Formosa talk about the martyrdom of
Christians on the mainland of China, and on that day I
speak on Matthew 5 : 11 and 12, " 'Blessed are ye, when men
shall revile you, and persecute you. . . . Rejoice, and be
exceeding glad : for great is your reward in heaven : for so
persecuted they the prophets which were before you.' There
is just one condition for strength for martyrdom, and that
is to be filled with the Holy Spirit. Do not fear the future.
Live for the moment. 'As thy days, so shall thy strength
be' (Deut. 33 : 25). When we are filled with the Holy Spirit
He gives us all the power and grace we need for the present
moment."

I see some with very unhappy faces as if they doubt what
I say.

"Perhaps it will help you when I tell you some of my own
experiences. During the last World War, I was in a prison
camp in Germany where the Bible was a forbidden book.
It was only by a miracle that I was able to smuggle my Bible

into the camp. When they searched us, I prayed to God to send angels to surround me, and although the woman in front of me and my sister behind me were both searched, I was not seen. This happened twice.

"When I entered the prison barracks I saw that 1,400 people were to be housed in a place built to accommodate 400. It was indescribably filthy, and soon there were many lice. This was a disaster in itself, but at the same time it all worked together for good, for the guards and officers would never come into our barracks, as they were afraid of getting lice from us. Consequently, we were able to have a Bible talk twice a day. For that purpose, God used angels and lice! God can use everything. And what a privilege it was to bring the happy Word of God to those poor despairing people—to tell them of Jesus Christ who had broken the vicious circle of sin and death when He died for us, and that He now lives for us.

"Once we were assigned a new forewoman, a fellow-prisoner who had to keep discipline in the barracks. Her name was Loni. She was a cruel woman who always had a leather belt in her hand with which to beat us, and she reported to the officers all we did. One day, when I opened my Bible, my friends whispered, 'Be careful; Loni is sitting behind you. If she sees your Bible, she will tell the guard, and then you will certainly be sent to the bunker.' The bunker was a cell from which people never came out alive. 'O Lord,' I prayed, asking for wisdom, 'You know that we cannot live without the light of Your Word in this dark prison. Protect us from Loni. Grant that she doesn't take away our Bible or tell the officers that we have one.' That prayer gave me the courage I needed. I read the Bible, prayed, gave my talk, and after that we sang 'Commit thy ways unto the Lord', a Dutch hymn.

"When we had finished singing we heard a voice, 'Another song like that.' It was Loni. She had enjoyed the singing, and we sang more on that day than we had sung on any day before. Later, I was able to talk with her, and show her the way of salvation. That was a happy ending.

"But I am no heroine. When you know that every word you say can mean a cruel death, then every word is as heavy as lead; but never before or since have I felt such joy and peace in my heart. God gave me grace to be a martyr. I do not at this moment need grace to be a martyr—I need only grace to speak to you and not be afraid of the spider which is sitting on the wall behind me, and which I hope will not creep into the sleeve of my coat." (Formosa has remarkably big spiders.) "But that I know from experience—if tomorrow, or next year, God should call upon me to be a martyr, He would give me all power and grace."

With my story, the ice is broken, and now several Formosans speak up. One says, "Once there were ten Chinese who were to be shot because they had courageously witnessed for Jesus Christ. Before the captain gave the command to shoot he said, 'If any of you want to save your lives, just renounce Jesus.' One Chinese stepped forward and renounced Jesus. Many people were watching, and immediately one of them jumped into the place where the man had been standing.

" 'What's the meaning of this?'

" 'I saw a crown falling, and I picked it up,' the Christian replied.

"Then came the command, 'FIRE!' Ten Chinese fell dead."

"Ten Chinese got martyrs' crowns," I commented, "and this is the greatest honour for a child of God."

It is as if a beam of light has made the darkness disappear. We go on talking about the honour of martyrdom. There is no fear left. The Holy Spirit has opened our eyes.

> I look not forward; God sees all the future,
> The road that short or long will lead me home;
> And He will face with me its every trial,
> And bear with me the burden that may come.

After the meeting an old woman says, "The spider is not in your sleeve; he disappeared into that hole in the wall."

CHAPTER XXVI

GOD'S EMBROIDERY

There is nothing too great for His power,
There is nothing too small for His love.

IN New Zealand are many immigrants from Holland. The first years are often difficult, especially for the unmarried ones. Family life has an even greater importance in this country than in the Fatherland, where there are so many other things to fill their lives. No Hollander at home can imagine the loneliness of life on the farms.

At a meeting I have spoken about answered prayers. The evening is warm, and before we go to bed we sit outside and have a little talk.

A young immigrant asks, "Can you really trouble God with the petty things of your life? I dare to speak with God about my soul, but I carry the sorrows of every day alone."

"Have you ever thought what God's love for us means? Love demands love, and don't you think that we can make God's father-heart happy by showing Him our love in telling Him of our cares? Earthly parents are happy when their children expect much from them. In Psalm 147:11 it says, 'The Lord taketh pleasure in those that hope in His mercy.' Don't forget that God sees our sorrows through our eyes. Imagine a little girl who comes crying to her mother because her doll is broken. Her mother doesn't say, 'Come along, don't be silly; that doll isn't worth a penny. What nonsense to cry about it.' No, she understands perfectly that the doll is the little one's sweetheart, and she tries to comfort her and says, 'Let us have a look and see if we can mend the doll.' Because she loves, she sees the catastrophe through the eyes of the child. God loves us more than an earthly father or mother. And His love makes our problems great in His eyes and small in our eyes.

"I will tell you something that happened when I was a prisoner in a concentration camp with my sister, Betsie.

One morning I had a terrible cold, and I said to Betsie, 'What can I do; I have no handkerchief.'

" 'Pray,' she said. I smiled, but she prayed, 'Father, Corrie has got a cold, and she has no handkerchief. Will You give her one in Jesus' name, Amen.'

"I could not help laughing, but as she said 'Amen', I heard my name called. I went to the window, and there stood my friend who worked in the prison hospital.

" 'Quickly, quickly! Take this little package; it is a little present for you.' I opened the package, and inside was a handkerchief.

" 'Why in the world did you bring me this? Did I ask you for it? Did you know that I have a cold?'

" 'No, but I was folding handkerchiefs in the hospital, and a voice in my heart said, "Take one to Corrie ten Boom." '

"What a miracle! Can you understand what that handkerchief told me at that moment? It told me that in heaven there is a loving Father who hears when one of His children on this very small planet asks for an impossible little thing—a handkerchief. And that heavenly Father tells one of His other children to take one to Corrie ten Boom. We cannot understand, but the foolishness of God is so much higher than the wisdom of the wise. With God, proportions are so different from ours. Perhaps in His eyes New Zealand is just as unimportant as a handkerchief. Perhaps in His eyes a handkerchief is just as important as New Zealand. I don't know. But this I do know : God answers prayers, and God's promises are a greater reality than our problems."

"Does God always grant us what we ask for in prayer?"

"Not always. Sometimes He says, 'No.' That is because God knows what we do not know. God knows all. Look at this piece of embroidery. The wrong side is chaos. But look at the beautiful picture on the other side—the right side.

> My life is but a weaving, between my God and me,
> I do not choose the colours, He worketh steadily,
> Ofttimes He weaveth sorrow, and I in foolish pride,
> Forget He sees the upper, and I the underside.
> Not till the loom is silent, and shuttles cease to fly,
> Will God unroll the canvas and explain the reason why.
> The dark threads are as needful in the skilful Weaver's hand,
> As the threads of gold and silver in the pattern He has planned.

"We see now the wrong side; God sees His side all the

time. One day we shall see the embroidery from His side, and thank Him for every answered and unanswered prayer. But even now, God gives us an answer in the Bible so that we can see His pattern in the great lines. For instance, to those who love God, all things work together for good. Faith is like radar which sees straight through the fog; the reality of things at a distance that the human eye cannot see.

"When I was in a prison camp in Holland during the last World War I often prayed : 'Lord, never let the enemy put me in a German concentration camp.' God answered 'No' to that prayer, but in the German camp we were among many prisoners who had never heard of Jesus Christ. If God had not used Betsie and me to bring them to Him, they would never have heard of Him. Many of them died, or were killed, but many died with the name of Jesus on their lips. They were well worth all our suffering, even Betsie's death. To be used to save souls for eternity is worth living and dying. In that way we saw God's side, and could thank Him for the unanswered prayer.

"The joyful thing is that all the time we have to fight the fight of faith, God sees His side of the embroidery. God has no problems concerning our lives—only plans. There is no panic in heaven. And I surely believe that one day when we are with the Lord we shall look back over the ages and see the whole world's history. Then we shall see and understand God's pattern for this world, but already, even now, God has allowed us to know His plan.

"In Ephesians 1 we read in Phillips' translation, 'God has allowed us to know the secret of His plan, and it is this : He purposes in His sovereign will that all human history shall be consummated in Christ, that everything that exists in heaven or earth shall find its perfection and fulfilment in Him. And here is the staggering thing—that in all which will one day belong to Him, we have been promised a share.'

"In England there was once a king who was to be crowned. He asked, 'Where will my bride stand during the coronation?' The answer was, 'It is the tradition that your bride may not stand beside you.' The king replied, 'I will not be crowned without her.'

"Do you know that of the Coronation day of the King of Kings, Jesus says the same? 'I will not be crowned without my bride.'

"That is the staggering thing, that in all which will one day belong to Him, we have been promised a share. The best is yet to be."

CHAPTER XXVII

TRAVEL ADVENTURES

Where He leads me I can safely go,
And in the blest hereafter I shall know
Why in His wisdom He hath led me so.

ONE takes no risk trusting God; trusting man can at times be very hazardous. Hudson Taylor said, "Why ask the help of impotent man, when we have an almighty God?" Gloriously certain it is that my missionary journeys, my retreat in Bloemendaal, and my refugee camp in Darmstadt all depend entirely on God. The message to me has been very clear that I must never ask for money. Often when I speak in churches, my hosts suggest an offering, but I never request one. In fact, I warn those who reject the message, whether it be a call to conversion or a commitment to Christ, not to give money. Satan sometimes suggests that an offering will satisfy God, when in fact He is demanding our all. Losing our life for Jesus' sake is an inescapable requirement. But how great is our gain! We are the great losers when we persuade ourselves that the giving of money is sufficient.

Hudson Taylor again reminds us, "We need not a great faith, but faith in a great God." Is my faith then always unwavering? No, indeed! It is Corrie ten Boom, she of little faith, who finding herself short of cash in Formosa, turns her purse inside out at least three times and once again balances her cheque-book.

Tomorrow I must make a short trip and pay the rent for my room. It is not a large sum I need, but it just is not there. Those very fine, helpful friends, shall I ask them? "May I not tell them, Father, that I need the money?" I pray. But the answer is plain, "Trust Me."

It is a busy day: three meetings and several talks with people. Tired out, I return to my room. My mail has come, twenty-six letters, the first to arrive in Formosa. There is not

time to read them all now, but out of the first one I open
falls a cheque for £50!

The next morning I open more letters. One tells of a
Christmas offering so generous that I can travel half-way
round the world. At the travel bureau I order my ticket.
"Please arrange flights for me from Formosa to the Philip-
pine Islands; to Auckland, New Zealand; to Sydney, Australia; to Johannesburg, South Africa; to Tel Aviv, Israel;
to Barcelona, Spain; to Amsterdam, Holland."

The clerk, a Chinese woman, writes out my itinerary.
"What is your final destination?" she asks.

"Heaven," I reply.

"How do you spell that?"

I spell it out, "H-E-A-V-E-N."

She smiles and says, "No, I don't mean that."

"But I mean it," I retort, "but you do not need to prepare
a ticket for me. I already have my reservation." She looks
at me inquiringly. "About 2,000 years ago the Lord Jesus
died on the cross to prepare a place in heaven for me. All
I needed to do was accept the ticket."

"That's true," says a Chinese who happens to pass by.
He is an employee in the office.

I ask him, "Do you have your reservation for heaven?"

"Indeed, I have," he replied. "I received Jesus Christ as
my Saviour, and He has made me a child of God. Every
child of God has a reservation in the house of the Father."

"Then there is something for you to do. This young lady
has no ticket. Please see to it that she does not come too
late."

Again I turn to the young woman and say, "I experience
great difficulties when I try to make flights for which I have
no reservations. But you meet much greater difficulties if you
have made no advance reservations for heaven. We are
told in John 1 : 12, as many as receive the Lord Jesus, to
them He gives power to become children of God. In John
14 : 2, 3, Jesus says, 'I go to prepare a place for you. . . . I
will come again, and receive you unto Myself; that where
I am, there ye may be also.' You see, He even provides the
transport."

When I get my ticket I see the route has been changed
to Sydney, Tel Aviv, Johannesburg. The clerk explains there

are no direct connections between Australia and South Africa. The stretch over the Indian Ocean is too long. "We need an island for landing purposes."

Laughing, I say, "Well, we'll have to pray for a little island in the Indian Ocean, for my route is Australia, South Africa, and then Tel Aviv."

Later she telephones me and asks, "Did you pray for an island? There is one after all. I have just heard that Qantas Airlines began a direct route between Melbourne and Johannesburg last month, and it uses the Cocos Islands, so you can follow your original travel plan."

When I arrive in Sydney I hear that the trip will take four days. All I need is packed into one bag, plus literature, note-books, Bibles, and coloured slides. I have taken coloured pictures in many lands, and use them often in meetings. They are my most prized possession. The manuscripts with sermons and lectures are also very valuable to me. Though seldom reading my notes when I speak, I prefer to have them before me. I have been accused of ascending the platform with three Bibles and five note-books, but it is hardly that bad. Meeting so many people, one hears a wealth of ideas, and I try to record as many as possible.

Walking towards the plane, a pilot offers to carry my bag. "That is too heavy for you. You can trust me; you will find it on your seat in the plane." But he heads in the wrong direction! He sees my anxiety. "Truly, madam, you can trust me. I'm just going to stop at the office. The bag will be on your seat."

But it is not on my seat! I check with the stewardess. We cannot locate the bag, but she assures me it has been stowed with the rest of the luggage. At Melbourne, however, I get a real jolt. A telephone message from Sydney announces that a bag belonging to Corrie ten Boom has been left behind.

"When can it be sent?"

"We can send it by plane to England, thence by plane to Italy, from there to Israel," and then a long list of stations and transfers from one air-line to another. My precious bag! It is not even locked! It contains all my earthly treasures. I am unhappy and angry.

During the trip the stewardess and I have discussed what

it means to be a child of God saved through Christ Jesus. A display of anger will scarcely be a recommendation, so I swallow my sharp words and try to say cheerfully, "Well, it must be for some reason; nothing happens by chance." I am perfectly aware that this is no victory. It would be victory if I had no resentment at all.

The plane climbs and I prepare as well as possible for the night. How dependent one feels in a plane. I pray earnestly for protection and a safe journey. After a short nap I waken, and unmistakably smell fire. The other passengers are also awake, and soon the stewardess comes and says, "I have good news for you. We're returning to Sydney to pick up your bag."

"Yes, indeed good news for me. But, tell me, are we not in great danger?"

"No. We're just having hydraulic difficulties. We'll stop for repairs while in Sydney."

Later it becomes clear what the hydraulic difficulties were. All the mechanism that depends on the hydraulic system no longer functions. The landing-gear has to be let down by turning a crank. The co-pilot stands before a window holding a flashlight. And every five minutes we are assured over the microphone, "There's absolutely no danger; we shall land safely."

I think, "Methinks thou dost protest too much," and am not reassured at all. Below is the sea. A plane, after all, is a very little thing. Where could we go in case of fire?

I am not afraid of death. Too often when a prisoner I had to face it. Moody said, "The valley of the shadow holds no darkness for the child of God. There must be light, else there could be no shadow. Jesus is the light. He has overcome death."

I pray, "Dear Lord, perhaps I shall see You very soon. I thank you for everything." My life passes before me as a panorama. How glorious to know that all my sins have been cleansed in the blood of the Lamb. "Promoted to Glory" was written in the death-notice of a Salvation Army soldier. O death, where is thy sting? O grave, where is thy victory? I thank my God for the victory of Jesus Christ.

Then suddenly I think of the others aboard. Are they prepared to die? I pray, "Lord, spare us, prolong the day of mercy for those that do not know You yet. Let us land safely." Looking about me, it is remarkable how the others react. There is no sign of panic. But no one sleeps; all sit quietly in their seats. The ladies are busy applying lipstick or powdering their noses.

I ask the woman beside me, "Do you feel it is important to enter eternity with painted lips?"

"What do you mean?" she asks.

"We are all aware that if this fire continues our lives are in danger."

"Oh, it's just that I don't feel completely dressed if I haven't touched up my lips."

At that moment I feel an urge to stand up and say to the people around me, "Friends, perhaps in a few moments we shall all enter eternity. Do you know where you are going? Are you prepared to appear before God? There is still time to accept the Lord Jesus as your Saviour. He died on the cross to carry the sins of the whole world, yours included. Believe on Him and you will be saved. He is able to grant eternal life." I know that I should say that, but I do not. In that critical moment I am ashamed of the Gospel of our Lord Jesus Christ. There is fear of man in my heart.

I cannot say that we land normally in Sydney, but we all get out safely. We are delayed for two days, so rooms are secured for us in a good hotel. Now there is time to do anything we please. My bag is returned to me, but there is no joy in my heart. I am ashamed.

"Dear Lord, send someone else; I am not fit to be a missionary. With so many others I stood before the very portals of eternity and warned no one. Send me back home, Lord. Let me repair watches. I am not worthy to be Your evangelist."

I read on the margin of one of my note-books something I had written down, "To travel through the desert with others, to suffer thirst, to find a spring, to drink of it, and not tell the others that they may be spared is exactly the same as enjoying Christ and not telling others about Him."

Later in the lounge a Jewish doctor approaches me and asks, "Do you know fear?"

"Yes, indeed. Very often I have been afraid."

"But you were not afraid tonight. I watched you all those

hours we were in danger of our lives, but you were neither anxious nor afraid. What is your secret?"

A ray of light! Perhaps after all! I tell him, "I am a Christian. I know the Messiah, Jesus, the Son of God, has come. He died on the cross for the sins of the world, your sins and mine. We read in the Bible, 'As many as received Him, to them gave He power to become the sons of God,' and I have accepted Him. If our burning plane had fallen into the sea I had the assurance of going to heaven. Jesus has said, 'In My Father's house are many mansions: I go to prepare a place for you.' And not only has He died for me; He has also promised that in His name I have power to withstand the evil one. Whenever fear welled up in my heart this evening, I said, 'In Jesus' name, depart.' Even Satan gives way before that name. 'All power in heaven and in earth' is at the back of that name."

The Jewish doctor returns four times, and each time his request is the same, "Tell me more about Jesus."

Found worthy to evangelise, after all! In this world to be acceptable we must pass examinations. God sometimes requires that we fail the examination, and only then will He use us. Paul says, "When I am weak, then am I strong" (2 Cor. 12:10). Thus one learns that without Him one can do nothing, but "I can do all things through Christ which strengtheneth me" (Phil. 4:13).

The great sin of negligence I confess to Him who is faithful and just to forgive our sins and to cleanse us from all unrighteousness (1 John 1:9).

CHAPTER XXVIII

THE OLD BOER

*As victory is the result of Christ's life lived out in the
believer, it is imperative that we see clearly that victory,
not defeat, is God's purpose for His children.*

IN South Africa I am associated for a time with Dr. J.
Edwin Orr. There is much I can learn from that lively,
world-wide evangelist, with his great gift of teaching and
his delightful Irish humour. I ask him not to arrange any
meetings for eight evenings so that I may listen to him.

One night he speaks from Phillips' translation of 1 Corinthians 3:14: "If the work that a man has built upon the
Foundation stands this test, he will be rewarded." It is a
strange experience, for he talks about myself. He repeats
what I had said, " 'I hope never to return to Germany. I am
willing to work in any part of the world, but not there.'
And yet it was just there, where she had suffered in a concentration camp, that God sent her. She went; she brought
her enemies the message of the forgiveness of sins, and also
found many friends. Was she God's child while she was
disobedient? So many fear they are no longer His children
when as Christians they sin. When my boy disobeys me, is
he not still my son? Fortunately Corrie did not persist in
her disobedience, but went to Germany. Happily for her, or
she would have missed her reward in heaven." Then he
looks at me. "Come to the platform, Corrie, and give us
your testimony. You get ten minutes."

Thus I stand before a large gathering of people, many of
whom I later meet, and soon there are many invitations to
speak.

One evening while speaking of the love we must bear our
enemies, I tell the story of Carl. I can see by the faces of
those before me that the Holy Spirit is at work. After the
meeting a Boer comes to me.

"Fifty years ago I saw the British murder my children,"
he says, "and for fifty long years I have struggled against

my hatred. Fifty long years I have tried to love my enemies, but never have I succeeded. Today I have seen the way. It is Jesus! What He has done for you He can do for me. He is the only One."

Had this been the only man for whom I had come to South Africa it would have been worth all the effort and expense. Jesus is the answer for South Africa with all its tensions and problems.

KAFFIR CABIN

A meeting is held in a cottage in a Negro village. Young and old are packed into two small rooms. I stand in the doorway between the rooms and speak of Jesus' love and His suffering on the Cross. A tiny girl of six supports the head of her sleeping baby sister as she sits on the bench beside her. The small rooms are hot and airless, and before long the little six-year-old also falls asleep. The little hand that bolstered the baby relaxes, and the baby tumbles to the floor with a bang, severely bumping her head. She screams at the top of her voice. Such a fall can be dangerous. It frightens me, and before I proceed, I pray, "O Lord, touch that little child with Your healing hand." At once the little one is quiet. Her father gathers her in his arms, and she goes calmly back to sleep.

CHAPTER XXIX

SPIRITUAL PRIDE

Most of us are cowards and compromisers. We will not face our sins. Christ came to lift us out of the old vicious circle of sin and death.

A YOUNG naval cadet comes to me with his difficulties. "Perhaps you can understand my trouble. My life is dark; I see no light."

"Tell me your problems. Perhaps together we can find an answer."

"To begin with, I never seem to know when to witness. One moment I speak up and spare no one, but an instant later when I should be witnessing, I am silent."

"You are a branch of the Vine. Imagine a branch that is cut off still trying to bear fruit. How foolish! You must be united with the Vine, the Lord Jesus, then *He* will bring forth the fruit."

"But how can I be in constant union with the Vine?"

"The Bible says, 'Be filled with the Spirit.' The Holy Spirit wants to live in your heart. 'He is ready to enter the heart of any child of God, just as light enters any room that is opened to it,' says Amy Carmichael. But there is no room for Him in a heart that is filled with sin. First you must have a clean heart."

"That's it exactly. For example, take my pride. I don't want to be proud, but there it is, always in my way. I am a minister's son, and because of that I feel I should really be a very good witness for Christ; but it is really my pride."

"Do you think your pride will disappear just because you wish it? Jesus died on the cross to deal with our sin problems. Look, I have with me a torch which does not light. I open it and pull out a piece of rag labelled 'pride'. Then others labelled 'worry', 'discouragement', 'inferiority', also, 'adultery' and 'dishonesty'. Finally, a yellow one stamped 'hatred'. All these in beside the batteries—small wonder the torch did not work. All the rags must come out to make room for the third battery. Thus, only in a clean heart is there room for the Holy Spirit.

"How wonderful to have the answer to the sin-problems. 'If we confess our sins, He is faithful and just to forgive us our sins, and to cleanse us from all unrighteousness. The blood of Jesus Christ, God's Son, cleanseth us from all sin' (1 John 1 : 9, 7). His blood does not cleanse excuses, only sins confessed. The two batteries in the flashlight, represent Conversion and Rebirth. First, there is a decision we must make, the first battery. In John 1 : 12 we read, 'As many as received Him, to them gave He power to become the sons of God.' That is easily understood. Even an earthly lawyer transacts no business for anyone who has not shown enough faith in him to give him a commission. Then, when we accept the Lord, that very important thing happens of which He speaks : we are 'born again'. Born into the very family of God, the second battery. Then we are God's children.

"I could never be a princess of the House of Orange, though I were to spend millions, or study at a hundred universities. A princess is born a princess, and a child of God must be born a child of God—'Born again,' says Jesus. The moment we say 'Yes' to the Lord Jesus, the Holy Spirit performs the gracious miracle of the rebirth. The moment we are born into the very family of God all promises of the Bible are written in our names and signed by Jesus Christ. We have not to start at the bottom but at the height where Jesus finished at the cross.

"One of the riches inherited through these promises is that Jesus said, "I will send the Comforter, the Holy Spirit, unto you'; and the most joyful commandment is, 'Be filled with the Spirit.' "

"The third battery is the fulness of the Holy Spirit. We must confess our sins. He forgives and cleanses, whereupon we praise the Lord and give thanks. The Holy Spirit will fill every heart that is cleansed by the blood of Jesus.

"Look, there are now three batteries in the torch, and it gives light."

"That all sounds very wonderful, but during my Quiet Time I am always so busy with the sins I uncover that little time is left for praise and thanksgiving."

"That's another of Satan's devices, making us introspective. If we look within ourselves we are bound to find more and more sin. Paul advises us in Hebrews 12 : 2 to look unto Jesus the author and finisher of our faith. Why not pray with the Psalmist, 'Search me, O God, and know my heart.' He will show you your sins. Not all of them at once, but increasingly you will recognise them, and always in the light of Christ's finished work upon the cross. Then God makes it very clear where you have to make restitution, and so you get right with God and right with men. To the end of our lives it remains a struggle against sin, but a victorious struggle. If only we put on the whole armour of God (Eph. 6 : 11–18), we go from victory to victory. Clear the decks of your sins. Be filled with the Spirit and with the fruit of the Spirit which is love, joy, peace, long-suffering, gentleness, goodness, faith, meekness, temperance (Gal. 5 : 22–23)."

"I had more problems I wanted to talk over with you, but I see the answer now. I have lived like a beggar when I am indeed a King's child."

"Yes. We are what we are in Jesus Christ. God has 'made Him to be sin for us, who knew no sin; that we might be made the righteousness of God in Him' (2 Cor. 5 : 21)."

CHAPTER XXX

TRUTH IS SO SIMPLE

*"There is joy in the presence of the angels of God over
one sinner that repenteth."*—Luke 15 : 10.

In the Post Office in Johannesburg is held a weekly Bible
meeting. The walls of the beautiful lecture room resound
to the music of Christian hymns. Christians meet there together, and invite all their workmates; a tremendous chance
for the Gospel. I find it to be the same in many towns in
South Africa, Christians also gathering in railway buildings
and insurance offices during lunch hours.

After I have spoken, a girl who has a free afternoon
brings me home. In the car we talk about the meeting.

"Do you know," she says, "I go every week to the lunch-
hour meeting and listen with great interest, but I have never
made the decision to become a Christian."

"Have you time to stop for a moment near that kopje?
I would like to show you something in my Bible."

We park in the shade of a tree. I open the Bible and
read Isaiah 53 : 6, " 'All we like sheep have gone astray;
we have turned every one to his own way.' Have you gone
God's way or your own?"

"My own way."

"We have all done that, but it is good that you know it.
If you didn't know it, I could hardly give you advice. Now
read on, 'The Lord hath laid on Him the iniquity of us all.' "

I take a book in my right hand, and lay it on my left.

"Look, God has taken your sins and laid them on His
Son, Jesus Christ, just as I have laid this book on my left
hand. This morning you heard how Jesus died on the cross
to carry the sins of all of us—the Lamb of God that taketh
away the sins of the world."

We read together John 1 : 12, "As many as received Him,
to them gave He power to become the sons of God, even to
them that believe on His name."

"Now, what is written there? Does He give the power to

become a child of God to those who try to be good and live a better life, or to those who are members of a church? No; only to those who receive Jesus. I say again, will you receive Him now? Jesus finished all that had to be done to make the barrier of sin disappear. Because of that God will forgive you."

She closes her eyes and prays, "Lord Jesus, will You forgive my sins? I receive you now as my Saviour and Lord."

"Now we will read John 1 : 12 again. What are you now?"

"A child of God," she replies.

"Will you thank Him for that?"

Again she closes her eyes, "Thank you, Lord Jesus, for saving me, and making me a child of God." Then she says, "What a joy now that I know it for sure. I really feel that I am now God's child."

"How often I have experienced that when we praise and give thanks the Holy Spirit witnesses with our spirit that we are children of God. This is a joyful beginning for you. Now go forward. Read your Bible faithfully. It is your book—about you and written for you. Confess all your sins to Him who will forgive and cleanse you. Not just sins in general, but mention the ones that the Lord shows you.

"The next thing is to join a church. This is not the foundation, for you are a child of God because you have accepted Jesus, but we need nourishing and teaching, and fellowship with other children of God. The Bible says in Hebrews 10 : 25 'Not forsaking the assembling of ourselves together, as the manner of some is', or as Phillips' translation puts it, 'Let us not hold aloof from our church meetings as some do.' "

On the way home she says, "How simple the way is, really."

"Yes. Complications are put there by you and me and the devil. The truth is simple, but so deep that we need the Holy Spirit to see the truth in its simplicity."

CHAPTER XXXI

GOSSIPING

It is just as bad to be drunk with gossiping as with liquor. Gossip is the most insidious of all the compensations for an inferiority complex. It is not only a sin— it is paranoid.

In a students' summer camp, we sit together to talk over the day. It is really time to go to bed, but the evening is hot. Above the lake the crescent moon shines. The Southern Cross is just above the horizon. Some of the constellations are the same as we see in Holland, but their angles are a little bit different.

We talk over the happenings of the day, and a witty student criticises the speakers of the conference. Her remarks are so accurate that we have to agree with her, and there is a lot of banter, but at the same time something of the joyful day is spoiled.

Sitting next to me is Shirley, a quiet and rather nervous girl We don't really know her yet, but now, when there is a lull in the conversation, I ask her a question in order to distract the others from their negative talking.

"Tell us something of your life, Shirley."

She waits a moment, and it almost seems as if she is too shy to speak. But then she starts to talk.

"You know, I never planned to study law. When I was a child, my ideal was to be a nurse, and I went to a big hospital as a student. In our spare time we often went to a nearby beach. I always felt myself to be the least of all those clever nurses, and I had the terrible feeling that everything I said and did was wrong. I could not get myself in tune with the others. Many of them would talk about other people, saying how boring or difficult the patients were, and heavily criticising the older nurses, and they always had something shocking to say about the moral lives of the doctors.

"One day they asked my opinion of a newly arrived

student nurse. I was flattered at being asked, and told them all the stupid things that the poor girl had done during her first week in the hospital. Suddenly I realised that everyone was listening to me; I exaggerated here and there so that my gossip became slander. But I was successful in gaining their attention and a little limelight. One of the girls said, 'Say, mouse, there is more behind that quiet face of yours than I had thought.'

"The next day I was working with the newcomer, and I saw many more of her mistakes and faults. Sometimes my friends of the beach looked at me knowingly when she did something stupid. For six weeks things went all right—no, I must say all wrong. I became more popular, and the new girl more nervous, and after a very sharp reprimand from one of the older nurses she left, and went home; later she became a patient in a mental institution. After she had gone I really understood what a terrible wrong I had done. I decided I would never again speak negatively, but I could not row against the tide in the hospital, so I left, and decided to study law."

"I fear that you will be a bad lawyer if you are always going to speak positively and never negatively," says one the boys.

"I am not afraid of that. It is one thing to see something wrong and to fight it with a positive purpose, and quite another to talk of wrong things in order to become popular and help the ego a little."

The conversation becomes general. I tell them how years ago in a girls' summer camp the atmosphere was almost spoiled by the campers because of their negative talking about each other. So we made a camp rule that before saying something negative we had to mention ten virtues of the person concerned. Sometimes it was impossible to find ten virtues, and so the negative thing could not be told. In the event of being able to find ten virtues, we would be so impressed at having done so that it seemed a pity to mention the negative at all !

One student tells us that in her campus, if anyone gossiped during meals, someone would say, "Pass the salt." That was the code words to warn people that gossip was abroad. This idea is very simple and practical.

After that a boy reads from Phillips' *Letters to Young Churches*, Romans, chapter 14, "Welcome a man whose faith is weak, but not with the idea of arguing over his scruples. After all, who are you to criticise the servant of somebody else, especially when that Somebody Else is God? It is to his own Master that he gives, or fails to give, satisfactory service. And don't doubt that satisfaction, for God is well able to transform men into servants who are satisfactory. Why, then, criticise your brother's actions, why try to make him look small? We shall all be judged one day, not by each other's standards or even our own, but by the standard of Christ. It is to God alone that we have to answer for our actions."

In Ephesians 4 : 30–32 (Phillips), Paul writes, "Let there be no more resentment, no more anger or temper, no more violent self-assertiveness, no more slander and no more malicious remarks. Be kind to each other, be understanding. Be as ready to forgive others as God for Christ's sake has forgiven you."

How clearly the Lord Jesus tells us in His Sermon on the Mount, "Judge not, that ye be not judged."

One of the girls comments, "I am so thankful that we have spoken about these things. I have never seen so clearly that gossiping is just the opposite to what the Bible teaches. We would be afraid of stealing money from each other, but we don't think anything at all of stealing somebody's good name, and I don't know which is worse. What can we do to stop it?"

"I think that Psalm 141 : 3 gives the answer, 'Set a watch, O Lord, before my mouth; keep the door of my lips.' People who throw mud have always got dirty hands. You cannot whiten yourself by blackening others. Be patient with the faults of others—they have to be patient with you.

"Before speaking, first think : Is it true, is it kind, is it necessary? If not, let it be left unsaid.

"When you point your finger at somebody, remember the other three fingers point back at yourself."

CHAPTER XXXII

THREE LETTERS

"Those who criticise us are the unpaid guardians of our souls. If what they say is true, do something about it; if it is not, forget it."—Stanley Jones.

MY programme is not always clearly mapped out. The most important thing is to go where God guides. If the green light is showing, then courageously cross the street. If the light shows red, then wait obediently. Sometimes there are moments when I do not see the way. I am to attend conferences, but the dates are so arranged that I have two months free in between. I am in England and have not yet made many contacts. A minister invites me to go with him to his parish, which is one of those old English towns with many boarding-schools. The invitation seems to be very attractive, as I can reach the same people for two months, join the life in a parish, and learn from those who must always work in the same area. I thankfully accept the invitation.

On the first day there is no work, and being alone in my room, I find a very welcome opportunity for quiet time and Bible study. But at the end of a week there is still no work. I am unable to make any personal contacts. When any visitors come to the house my lunch is sent to me in my room. I do not know if there is really any activity in this parish—if there is I do not see it.

The minister and his wife are very kind, but I feel some opposition from them, and it is a strange experience for me to have to sit and wait. In many countries there is work for me. Sometimes the programmes are so heavy that to answer all the invitations and fit everything in can be a real puzzle.

I search my heart to see if I am offended. One can so easily become too great to be used by God. One can never be too small for His service. Just then I receive a letter from a friend in Holland. He writes, "Corrie, your whole work is nothing but a flash in the pan. All this wandering over the world is just a means of finding adventure. You do so many wrong things that you lose the respect of other people, but that is what you deserve. The worst thing is that God's name is dishonoured by your behaviour."

Is this really so? How good it is that I have time to think it over, and to talk with my heavenly Father about it. I am used to confessing immediately when I am aware of sin. It is so certain that when we confess sin we experience that God is true and faithful, and that He forgives us our sins and cleanses us from all unrighteousness, that I very seldom think of the past. But now I have a spring cleaning. I pray, "Search me, O God, and know my heart : try me, and know my thoughts : and see if there be any wicked way in me, and lead me in the way everlasting." When the Holy Spirit shows us our sins, it is always in the light of the finished work at Calvary. Sanctification is not a heavy yoke, but a joyful liberation.

The next day another letter arrives. This one is from a family with whom I spent a week as their guest—a retired prison governor from India with his two daughters. "God has so blessed your visit to us, that my daughters and I have been born again. Now all three of us are going to work for the Lord. I am going back to India, where I served the world for so long, and where in future I shall serve God. I know the language of the Indians, and I will spend the last years of my life living with them and bringing them the Gospel."

That evening I pray, "Lord, I am a branch of the Vine— nothing more, and nothing less. Give me tomorrow two souls to save as a sign that You can still use me."

The following morning the third letter arrives. It is from a young woman. She tells me, "God used your words to awaken me. I am now much more active. Today I had the joyful experience of bringing two girls to the Lord."

That is the answer. Indirectly God has used me for two souls. I can go on quietly. God works.

During the last week of my stay in the place the minister changes his attitude. He brings me into contact with schools, clubs, and a home for soldiers. The quiet time has gone, but what a blessing it has been. After this attack, I go on in greater dependence on Him who is our Vine. Without Him we can do nothing : with Him we are more than conquerors.

CHAPTER XXXIII

READY FOR THE SECOND COMING OF JESUS

The restless millions await the coming of the light that maketh all things new. Christ also waits, but men are slow and few. Have we done all we can? Have I? Have you?

"CHANGED people make changed cities; changed cities make changed countries; changed countries make a changed world," says a young minister.

We are at a house party in England. Many young people listen to his words. I look around me. Some people remain indifferent; others are full of enthusiasm. Is this the answer for the problems of our time, this atomic age, when the world is approaching the greatest crisis in history?

When I am alone with the young minister afterwards, I ask him, "Do you really believe what you said? I don't believe it is true. The time of grace is passing, and the world will not be changed by changed people. When the time of the Gentiles is fulfilled and Jesus returns, He has promised, 'I make all things new' (Rev. 21 : 5). I certainly hope that revival will come throughout the whole world, and that God will use it to bring in the fulness of the Gentiles, for revival is the true preparation for the Second Coming. That is why every Christian must be an evangelist as far as the opportunity is given to him by God. Then the coming of this time will be speed up. As it says in 1 John 3 : 3, 'Every man that hath this hope in him purifieth himself, even as He is pure.'

"It is truth that makes one free, not idealism. The expectation of the Second Coming of the Lord changes people from being earthbound to people whose eyes are focused on the future of the Lord, and gloriously opened to the great value of bringing the happy tidings to this poor world. They see that bringing people to Jesus Christ is the most important work for every child of God."

"I do not understand why you believe so strongly that Jesus is going to come again soon. Surely He comes into our hearts when we trust Him, and again in the hour of our death."

"The angel said differently. In Acts 1:11 it is written that when the disciples looked with amazement towards the clouds after the ascension, the angel told them, 'This same Jesus, which is taken up from you into heaven, shall so come in like manner as ye have seen Him go into heaven.' It doesn't say anything there about the coming of the Lord into our hearts or the hour of our death, but His coming on the clouds of heaven."

"All right; but so many before have expected His coming again. In crises throughout the world's history there has always been an escape for Christians in their expectations of Christ's return, and yet things have continued as they always have done from the start of creation."

"Peter has said exactly the same. In his second epistle, chapter 3 and verses 3 and 4, he writes, 'Knowing this first, that there shall come in the last days scoffers, walking after their own lusts, and saying, Where is the promise of His coming? for since the fathers fell asleep, all things continue as they were from the beginning of the creation.' Search your heart. If there is a tendency to walk after your own lust, if there is love for earthly things, if you will not lose your self, your ego, then, of course, there will be doubt of the Lord's Second Coming. It is then that you will try to put forward logical and theological arguments. Study your Bible in obedience, and you will find many details.

"God's Word teaches us far more about Jesus' second coming than about any other truth, and it is about this that Christians know so little. That is partly the fault of the ministers, who perhaps mention the Second Coming in one sentence at the end of a sermon, or in the catechism once a year. But every Christian has God's Word, which can tell them very much about the future. The most important thing for a Christian to consider is his attitude, his being prepared. Jesus tells us about the wise virgins with oil in their lamps. Does oil here mean the Holy Spirit? When we are filled with His Spirit instead of love for our own lusts, then we are ready and can follow the advice of John when he says in his first epistle, "Abide in Him; that, when He shall appear, we may have confidence, and not be ashamed before Him at His coming.'

"I believe that God is opening the eyes of the theologians to the great importance of this truth. One of the atomic scientists told Professor Karl Barth that they are prisoners of science and politics, and asked him how the problem could be solved. Professor Barth replied that the only answer is the Second Coming of the Lord Jesus. He was right. When Jesus does what He has promised in Revelation 21 : 5, to make everything new, then swords will be changed into ploughshares, and atomic power will be used to build up instead of to destroy.

"Have you read my book *A Prisoner and Yet . . .?* In it you can see that Jesus' light is stronger than the deepest darkness. Only those who have had the experience of being in a concentration camp can know how deep that darkness really is. No matter how deep down into darkness one goes, deeper still are the everlasting arms. The Czechoslovakian, Giorgiu, wrote a book after he had had experiences similar to mine. Two people, both in a concentration camp; but that poor man had been there without Jesus Christ. I had Jesus Christ with me, and that made all the difference. He called his book *The 25th Hour.* In it he describes how he was once in a submarine where he was shown some white mice, and was told that when the mice died it meant that the oxygen was giving out, and unless the submarine surfaced, the occupants would have only a few hours to live. Giorgiu writes, 'That moment has arrived in the world's history. The white mice have already died—it is a question of a very short time and then this planet will be finished. The day has twenty-four hours; we are in the twenty-fifth hour.' Is this nonsense, or is it true, that we live on a very dangerous planet where two or more countries have atomic bomb factories and worse? Henry Adams has said, 'We know so little, and our power is so great.' Are we really in the twenty-fifth hour? Now is the time for Christians to give the answer to a desperate world. The Bible is very clear in its description of the future. Those who read the newspapers and the Bible together know that we are approaching the time which Jesus spoke about, 'Look up, for your redemption draweth nigh' (Luke 21 : 28).''

"I know so little about the return of the Lord.''

"That is a sure sign that you don't read your Bible. Do you know that one out of every twenty-five texts in the New Testament is about the future, and that the Bible gives many details? Frederick the Great has said, 'When you want to know how late it is on the clock of world history, look at the Jews.' It is very clear that a tremendous thing started with the Jews when the State of Israel was born on the 14th May, 1948. It is at the same time one of the oldest and the youngest nations in the world, and it is not only those who understand the signs of the times who realise that we are approaching the greatest crisis in history, but everyone in the world.''

"But we have had times like that before. During the Thirty Years' War the Germans were preparing themselves for the Second Coming.''

"Yes, but now things are far more serious than ever before, and, look at the Jews.''

"But, tell me, are you really not scared about the Second Coming of the Lord?''

"No. I know what to do with my sins. When we confess them, God is faithful to forgive us our sins, and the blood of Jesus cleanses us from all sins confessed to Him. Those who have the hope that Jesus is coming soon purify themselves as He is pure, and that is possible because we can bring our sins to Him. The Bible tells us very clearly how to wait for His coming. In Titus 2 : 13 is written, 'Looking for that blessed hope, and the glorious appearing of the great God and our Saviour Jesus Christ.' Instead of looking for His appearing, too many Christians start arguing about it.

"But the millennium is mentioned clearly only once in the Bible.''

"How often must it be mentioned in God's Word before you believe it to be true? But I don't mind what you think about the millennium. It is far more important for you to see the Second Coming as a joyful event for all God's children. In Revelation 22 : 17 John says, 'And the Spirit and the bride say, "Come." And let him that heareth say,

"Come." ' When these three agree, then He will come quickly."

"But I dare not say 'Come' as long as I am not sure if I am ready."

"Do you hunger and thirst after righteousness so as to be ready for that day? Then read on, 'And let him that is athirst come. And whosoever will, let him take the water of life freely.' God has prepared it. We have only to receive it. God's promises are available on demand. Read 2 Corinthians 5 : 21, 'He hath made Him to be sin for us, who knew no sin, that we might be made the righteousness of God in Him.' "

"One other thing. I dare not long for Jesus to return when there are so many unsaved people in the world. How terrible it would be for them."

"Do you really mean that? Then don't ask the Lord Jesus to delay His coming, but go as soon as possible to the unsaved, and tell them the way of salvation, for the most important work in these last days is bringing the Gospel to everyone you can reach. The Lord Jesus, in Luke 19 : 13, says, 'Occupy till I come.' Paul tells us in 2 Timothy 4 : 8, 'Henceforth there is laid up for me a crown of righteousness, which the Lord, the righteous judge, shall give me at that day : and not to me only, but unto all them also that love His appearing.'

"You are concerned about those who are not ready. Do you realise that today there are more people not ready than yesterday; more children have been born all over the world than people have been reborn? So it is a little darker today than yesterday."

CHAPTER XXXIV

TRANSLATION OF THE CHURCH

I do not wait for the undertaker, but for the Uptaker.

ONE morning, a woman reads in her Bible (1 Thess. 4:13–18, Phillips), "Now we don't want you, my brothers, to be in any doubt about those who 'fall asleep' in death, or to grieve over them like men who have no hope. After all, if we believe that Jesus died and rose again from death, then we can believe that God will just as surely bring with Jesus all who are 'asleep' in Him. Here we have a definite message from the Lord. It is that those who are still living when He comes will not in any way precede those who have previously fallen asleep. One word of command, one shout from the Archangel, one blast from the trumpet of God and the Lord Himself will come down from heaven! Those who have died in Christ will be the first to rise, and then we who are still living on the earth will be swept up with them into the clouds to meet the Lord in the air. And after that we shall be with Him for ever. God has given me this message on the matter, so by all means use it to encourage one another."

As she reads, it speaks to her in a special way. The signs of the times are clear, and that great events are due to take place soon is evident, not only to Bible readers but to all who read the newspapers. So deeply is she buried in thought about the Lord's return for His own that she has no ears for the door-bell. After a while it registers, and she opens the door, still holding her Bible.

The milkman is waiting impatiently. "You must be getting deaf, madam. I had to ring three times."

"I'm sorry. It is not that I am deaf, but I have just read something in my Bible so glorious I forgot everything else. Do you know that it is possible that some day you may come to my door and I will be no longer here? Also you may find every Christian home empty. I've just read that when Jesus comes again we shall meet Him in the air. We shall be suddenly changed, and then we shall see Him face to face. You may not realise why people everywhere are missing. Later you may hear, and ask, 'Why didn't that old woman tell me before?' That is why I'm telling you now. But listen, Mr. Milkman, if you accept Jesus as your Saviour, you, too, will become a child of God and be among those who will meet Him in the air."

Whether or not we agree with the old lady's conclusions, we see that she knew what it meant to watch for the Lord's return.

"Can ye not discern the signs of the times?" (Matt. 16 : 3).

"When these things begin to come to pass, then look up . . . for your redemption draweth nigh" (Luke 21 : 28).

It will not be important that we have much money, but rather that we recognise at that reunion those for whom Christ sent us into this world, and to whom we have spoken of the way of salvation.

CHAPTER XXXV

ZONNEDUIN

The time is short—too short for listless dreaming
O'er vanished fancies fair.
Around the hearts are breaking, tears are streaming.
Thou art needed everywhere.

THIS evening a fresh breeze comes over the dunes and makes the air deliciously cool in the garden after the heat of the day. Although the sun has not yet set, I hear nightingales singing.

"How did you come to open this home?" an American visitor asks.

"My sister Betsie had a vision. She and I were in a prison camp in Germany where there were, among others, about one thousand Dutch people. She told me, 'God has said to me that we must help these people around us after the War. If they come out alive, they will find it difficult to find a way through life again. Their experiences here have affected their health, and there is a terrible darkness in the hearts of many—they are mentally sick. God will give us a beautiful house, with flowers and colours. There, many will find the way to life again. They will come in contact with the Gospel, and be found by Him who will be their Saviour and Lord, Jesus Christ, and who has the answer to all problems. As soon as the house is opened we must travel over the world with the Gospel to tell everyone who is willing to listen. We must tell them, too, that we have experienced that Jesus is Light in the deepest darkness.'

"Betsie died in the prison, but after the War I did what God had told her. Many Dutch people have been in this home—people who had been in prison or suffered in other ways from the War—but they are now back in their own homes again. It is now a home where everyone who needs a time of rest, or to spend a vacation, is welcome."

Zonneduin has become an international house. I have friends all over the world, and many come to visit Europe.

Holland is so small that people can get to know the whole country by making daily excursions from this house. Close by there is a wood and dunes and a scenic reserve where many plants and flowers can be found. Bloemendaal is a beautiful place for walks, but a young Swiss girl tells me, "The most glorious thing for me is that here in Zonneduin I have found my Saviour."

Holland is a beautiful country. There are countries where the scenery is mighty and expansive. Holland has its own special beauty. It is my Fatherland. It is not often that I am here, but when in Europe I try to come home for a time in between visits to other countries. I enjoy the far views of the fields, the blonde dunes, and the pine-trees of het Gooi, and in Zonneduin I have a room with my own pictures and paintings on the walls, and my own books in the bookcase.

"Why don't you stay here when you like it so much?" an English girl asks. "There is plenty of work for you here."

Before I answer, I am quiet for a moment, and listen to the song of the nightingale.

"My life doesn't belong to me. I must follow where the Lord leads. I was bought at a high price, and must be obedient to the One who purchased me."

"Isn't it costly to live like that?"

"Yes, but it is far more costly to disobey."

In my memory I see people in Bermuda behind bars—a tiny girl in Norton—a Boer in South Africa—school children in Cuba—lepers in Formosa. . . . "We need your message; come back again," they have said.

My ability is very limited, but I am no more and no less than a branch of the Vine. Without the Vine I cannot do anything. Connected with the Vine, He gives His branches His nature, His victory, His love, His power. With Him, more than conqueror. Not good if detached.

"Go ye therefore, and teach all nations" and "Make them my disciples," says Jesus.

"Now to Him who is able to keep you from falling and to present you before His glory without fault and with unspeakable joy, to the only wise God, our Saviour, be glory and majesty, power and authority, now and ever, Amen."

CONCLUSION

God has no grandchildren.

IN Mexico I asked a boy, "Are you a child of God?"
His answer was, "Señora, I go to church every Sunday."

"That is good, but not sufficient. When I go into a garage, I do not become a motor car. A mouse born in a biscuit tin does not become a biscuit. There is only one way to become a child of God—obey John 1 : 12. Those who receive Jesus as their Saviour and their Lord, He makes children of God."

"But my parents are fine children of God."

"God bless them, but don't forget that God has no grandchildren. After you have received Jesus as your Saviour, you are adopted into the very family of God, and you can say to Him with a happy heart, 'Father, my Father'" (Rom. 8 : 14).

The boy understood and made the decision that makes the angels rejoice.

And what about you who have read this book? Did you ever make this decision? If not, why not have a talk with the Lord Jesus and ask Him to enter into your heart? He has been knocking all the time you have been reading. And when you open the door He comes in (Rev. 3 : 20).

You are perhaps a faithful church member. But are you sure that you are a child of God? When a young man and a young woman have fellowship there can come a moment when he asks her, "Do you love me, and will you accept me as your husband?" The young woman does not answer, "I like your morals, and you give me such nice presents, and I love to talk with you." When things are all right the girl says, "Yes", and that is a decision for life.

Sometimes people answer me when I ask them to accept Jesus, "But I pray often, and I like the Sermon on the Mount." Do you think the Lord is satisfied with that? Jesus loves you very much, and that is why He wants your heart and the personal decision that is for time and eternity.

If you have, then read the Bible; it is your book, about

you, for you. Learn the words by heart. "As newborn babes, desire the sincere milk of the word, that ye may grow thereby" (1 Pet. 2 : 2). For the warfare of life you need the "sword of the Spirit". And that is the Word of God.

As well as memorising Scripture, I strongly advise you to commence a Bible study course. These are two of the most helpful and practical ways of growing as a Christian. The Navigators have an excellent Scripture memorising course as well as a Bible study course, both of which I can heartily recommend. Their addresses will be found on the next page.

You will never regret that you accepted Jesus as your Saviour and Lord. For ten years now I have travelled all over the world. I have met watchmakers who would have preferred to be farmers, and farmers who would rather have been watchmakers, soldiers who regretted not being in the Navy, and sailors who wished they were in the Army. I could go on and tell you about many frustrated people I have met. But never have I found any Christian who regretted having accepted the Lord Jesus as Saviour. And you will not, either. But now go on and take all the riches written on your name and signed by Jesus Christ.

He saves from the guilt, the penalty, the stain, and the dominion of sin.

How wonderful!

We are saved by the sovereign grace of God and the precious blood of Jesus.

How amazing!

He will make us instruments for the saving of others, that we might be to the praise of His glory.

How beautiful!

Jesus Christ opens wide the doors of the treasure-house of God's promises, and bids us go in and take with boldness the riches that are ours.

How great!

Jesus was Victor!

Jesus is Victor!

Jesus will be Victor!

Corrie ten Boom.

The addresses from which the Scripture memorising and Bible study courses can be obtained from are :

In Great Britain—

The Navigators,
89A The Broadway,
Wimbledon,
London, S.W.19.

In New Zealand—

The Navigators,
P.O. Box 1951,
Christchurch.

In U.S.A.—

The Navigators,
Colorado Springs,
Colorado, 80901.